KITCHEN EXPRESS

Good Food Fast—For Real People with Real Lives

by Dee Wolk—Creator of "The Weight Solution"

Illustrated by Mark Zeszotek—Emmy-Award-winning illustrator for Jim Henson Productions

Streamline Your Life
With Guiltless, Healthy Cooking
Without Sacrificing Time or Taste!

Featuring
The 20-Minute-Meal Deal!

QUAIL RIDGE PRESS

Copyright © 1997 by
Kitchen Express Books, Inc.

Third Edition

All rights reserved. No part of this publication may be reproduced or used in any form or by any means—
graphic, electronic, or mechanical, including photocopying, recording, taping or through information storage
and retrieval systems—without written permission of the author or publisher.

Kitchen Express is not intended to prescribe a diet or offer medical advice.
As with any change in your diet, please consult your physician.

Library of Congress Cataloging-in-Publication Data

Wolk, Dee, 1935-
  Kitchen express : good food fast, for real people with real lives : streamline your life with guiltless, healthy cooking without
scrificing time or taste! : featuring the 20-minute meal deal! / by Dee Wolk. -- 3rd ed.
     p.   cm.
  Includes index.
  ISBN 0-937552-77-1
  1. Quick and easy cookery.   2. Low-fat diet—Recipes.   I. Title
TX833.5.W65   1997
641.5'55—dc21

QUAIL RIDGE PRESS
P. O. Box 123 • Brandon, MS 39043
1 - 8 0 0 - 3 4 3 - 1 5 8 3

This book is dedicated to my husband, Craig Orum.
His support, commitment and love make everything possible.
Thanks, Honey!

ODE TO REAL PEOPLE
—TIRED, HUNGRY, REAL PEOPLE

Give me your tired, your overscheduled,
your overcommitted life situation

Your yearning to cook healthy and be carefree.

Your kitchen has become a wretched refuse
of pricey chemical contamination.

Come all you tired, hungry, discouraged masses unto me.

Let me show you how to prepare good food fast,
the key to your salvation.

—Dee Wolk

CONTENTS

Introduction 7

Foreword 10

Chapter One—GOOD FOOD FAST: HOW TO MAKE IT HAPPEN 11
   Formula: Two Hours in the Kitchen = One Month of Dinner Meals 13
   The Right Tools 14

Chapter Two—THE BIGGER PICTURE: BASIC COMMON SENSE NUTRITION 17
   What should I Eat? 18
   Nutrition Basics 19
   Make Small Changes 21
   Let's Talk About Fat 22
   Eat More Fiber 29
   Bone Up on Calcium 31
   Watch the Sugar 32
   Hold the Salt 34
   Alcohol 35
   Wrap-Up 36

Chapter Three—LET'S GO SHOPPING: A TRIP TO THE SUPERMARKET 37
Smart Shopping Tips 39
Food Labeling 41
Basic Low Fat Food List 43
Dee's Picks—Brand Name Food Favorites 46

Chapter Four—DEE'S KITCHEN EXPRESS RECIPES 51
Appetizers & More 53
Salads 65
Soups, Vegetables & Pasta 69
Poultry, Meat & Seafood 99
Desserts 129

Chapter Five—EXERCISE: THE KEY TO WELLNESS 139
Four Steps to an Effective Workout 142
The Workouts 149

Chapter Six—WRAP UP 153

Index 158

INTRODUCTION

It's impossible to talk about why I wrote this book without telling you a little about myself and the weight-loss workshops I began teaching over ten years ago. As a former fat person, I had tried almost every diet known to humankind—hundreds of different diets, many of them extremely unhealthy. If you can believe it, I even allowed myself to be injected with the urine of a pregnant cow—performed by a certified M.D.—all in the name of losing weight. No doubt, the diet world has progressed from that sad state—or has it?

Diets simply do not work. A diet is a temporary state of being—you're either on a diet or you're not. Diets are nothing more than band-aids and the diet industry is bleeding millions of people of precious resources—of their self-esteem, money and time.

After a lifetime of dieting failures, I embarked on a two-year journey of personal research. From this, I developed my weight loss workshop, a non-diet program to end all diets. My program ends the vicious cycle of dieting and regaining weight due to continuous obsession with food. Through the workshop, I have instructed thousands of people to enjoy the foods of their choice in moderation with ease and control, and still lose weight.

I believe in the power that lives in each of us. My program empowers people through building healthy self esteem, behavior modification and self-exploration. My clients averaged about a 2.5 pound weight loss per week; approximately 85% of my clients have maintained their weight loss permanently since taking my seminar. *Kitchen Express* evolved from the vast majority of my clients who didn't know their way around a kitchen—least of all, their own! They lacked not only the expertise, but also the time to cook. They knew the frozen food section of their supermarket better than they did their own kitchen.

Kitchen Express serves up the answer to this double bind: good, fresh food that's fast, easy to prepare, attractive on the plate and delicious to the palate. That's how this book was born. This book is magical. I don't mean to suggest that fairy dust is hidden within the pages. This book is magical because it's guaranteed to turn you into a wizard in your own kitchen.

Okay, I know what you're thinking. "I'm tired. I don't have the time or energy to get into something that will take more out of me!" WRONG! You don't know me well enough yet, but I wouldn't do that to you. I'm tired, too. Everyone is tired, many times even too tired to pop a frozen entrée into the microwave.

That's exactly why I wrote this book. I want you to unlock your culinary skill with a minimum of time and effort. I want to empower you in your own kitchen! I want you to stop eating unhealthy foods that are sapping you of more energy—what I call digging your grave with your teeth.

I want to teach you how to cook good food fast. Food that is free from chemical contamination. Food that is good for you. Food that is so easy to prepare, you'll have time leftover to be carefree. Food that is attractive on the plate and delicious to the palate. Food that will even increase your self-esteem.

Close your eyes for just a minute. Imagine opening your freezer or refrigerator to a variety of ready-to-heat specialties—free from food additives and chemicals—that took a minimum of time to prepare and freeze. Imagine lots of choices for you, for your family, for company, invited or unexpected. Good food fast, IN YOUR KITCHEN!

It's true! This book is the kiss of culinary efficiency and artistry—it will turn you into a wizard in your own kitchen. Ready to get started? Good! Let's catch the *Kitchen Express* and cook GOOD FOOD FAST! All aboard!

FOREWORD

It is a rare instance, indeed, when the principles of quick cooking can be happily married to a healthy approach to eating. *Kitchen Express* has managed to accomplish this daunting task with humor, fun, and a minimum of fuss. And the results are outstanding! How do I know? I've had the personal pleasure of dining in Dee's home and tasting some of the recipes that you, too, can now enjoy. Dee infuses her recipes with her passion for good food, attention to good nutrition, and with versatility that allows many of them to be served up several appetizing ways.

This cookbook is unique in that it makes large portions that can be frozen or kept for hectic times ... and best of all, they not only taste good, they are good for you! These delicious recipes allow you to keep a philosophy I have long embraced: "Eat More of the Best ... and Less of the Rest!"

By Susan L. Thom, RD, LD, CDE

Good Food Fast!

Chapter One

GOOD FOOD FAST:
HOW TO MAKE IT HAPPEN

They say that the first step to change is awareness. I agree. What are we aware of? Most of the fast food we purchase and ingest is pricey chemical contamination. The restaurant fast food we gobble on the run is high in fat and sodium, and forgettable in taste. Meals from the supermarket frozen food section, even those low-cal entrées, are riddled with chemicals and preservatives—and oh, so exciting, aren't they? Yeah, about as exciting as TV reruns.

We are aware of these things. We know that these foods are not good for our bodies. But we're too busy to prepare a meal; we're tired, and we don't know any other option. We'd like to make changes, but where do we start? And how?

Now that we've become aware of what we're doing, we need a plan to change—a strategy that will streamline our efforts in the kitchen and help us to become healthy, good cooks.

No one wants to cook when they're tired—it's fruitless (pardon the food pun!) and negative. Instead, I encourage you to cook when your energy level is up—like on the weekend. Cooking or pre-cooking and freezing is a way of life for me—a discipline that sets me free.

FORMULA:
TWO HOURS WELL SPENT IN THE KITCHEN = ONE MONTH OF DINNER MEALS

It's true. If you spend a moderate amount of time when you're relatively energetic preparing food for future meals, I guarantee you'll be able to open your freezer a week later, make a selection, and have something delicious to eat in 20 minutes.

Twenty minutes? Yes, I'm talking about 20 minutes per meal, from heating to table. **The 20-Minute-Meal Deal!** It can happen in your life. Without chemicals. Without coupons. Without waiting in the drive-through of your favorite fast food joint.

The recipes I've chosen in this book are healthy and preservative free. Several of them are completely fat free. Some are very low in fat; a few have what I would consider a moderate amount of fat. Wherever possible, I have modified the recipes to be low in fat, but still produce tasty, delicious food.

To help you lower dietary fat, decide how many fat grams you want to eat for the entire day. By doing this, you can occasionally choose foods that are higher in fat, because you've made lower-fat food choices previously that day. If you give yourself a fat allowance each day, you can allow yourself a higher fat meal that's within your daily fat gram bank—because you've budgeted for it.

My weight-loss program stresses moderation, not counting calories, weighing and measuring food, etc. I teach the importance of food satisfaction in my workshops. We learn to peacefully coexist with all foods. True food satisfaction helps to prevent cheating and binging. I believe that it's better to have a small portion of what I'm really craving than it is to eat a lot of low-calorie, tasteless food that I don't really want. When I really want a delicious pasta salad, that's what I choose to eat—not two cups of spinach without dressing, as may be prescribed by a diet.

THE RIGHT TOOLS

One key to our strategy is organization in the kitchen. This means having the right tools handy at your fingertips. Think about it. When you call a plumber, he arrives at your house with special tools to unclog your drain. When you take your car in for service, does your mechanic borrow tools from the garage down the street? Absolutely not! He has the tools he needs right there.

The tools I've listed here will get your act together, helping you to create good food fast. You probably have many of these items already—you just need to learn to depend on them! Most of them can be found in a housewares department or a discount housewares store.

TOOLS OF THE TRADE:

Appliances
- Toaster oven
- Microwave oven

Cookware
- Pasta pot, dutch oven, or stock pot—minimum 4-quart size
- Nonstick saucepans and skillets—assorted sizes

Kitchenware and must-haves
- Mixing bowls—assorted sizes
- Cutting board
- Lettuce/salad spinner
- Colander
- Garlic press
- Basting brush
- Can opener
- Hand grater
- Potholders
- Vegetable peeler
- Potato masher
- Spatula
- Rubber scraper
- Spoons—wooden and plastic

Bakeware and ovenware
- Cookie sheet
- Roasting rack

Cutlery and Measuring Tools
- Good knife set—including chef's knife, carving knife, serrated knife, paring knife and bread knife
- Measuring cups—assorted standard sizes
- Measuring spoons—assorted standard sizes

Paper products
- Paper towels
- Aluminum foil
- Zippered freezer bags with labels

AND, MOST IMPORTANT OF ALL—A GOOD, POSITIVE ATTITUDE!

We're not only going to become kitchen wizards, we're going to have fun while doing it!

Now that we've owned up to our bad eating habits and planned how we'll make changes, let's choo-choo on down to the next stop on our *Kitchen Express* odyssey. Ready to take action? It's a whistle-stop away!

Chapter Two

Nutrition

THE BIGGER PICTURE:
BASIC, COMMON SENSE NUTRITION

WHAT SHOULD I EAT?

Since there is no one perfect food with all the nutrients we need to sustain good health, I advocate eating a variety of foods, balanced from the five food groups. These groups are: 1) vegetables and fruits; 2) breads, cereals and other grain-based foods; 3) dairy products such as milk, yogurt and cheese; 4) proteins, including meat, fish, poultry, dry beans and peas; and 5) fats. AND WATER! Lots of water!

In my weight management program, I have never advocated diets. In fact, my program is subtitled, "The non-diet program to end all diets." And believe me, if I had my way, no one would ever go on a diet again to lose weight. I believe in eating all foods in moderation. This requires planning. Planning is the key for anyone, any life-style. It doesn't matter who you are or what you do—everyone needs a blueprint to help them ease into healthy foods.

Whenever I use the word "diet" in this book, diet means what you eat in a 24-hour period—not some calorie or food restricting program. By reviewing your daily diet, you can begin to plan ahead on how to juggle nutrient sources.

For example, if you intend to eat something relatively high in fat, such as pizza, you should eat other foods that day that are relatively lower in fat, such as cereal, veggies and fruits. Note that I didn't say you shouldn't have pizza—or anything else you may desire. I advocate eating what you want, but in moderation, balancing that food with other, healthier choices.

A word about moderation. Eating in moderation is the key to my eating plan. Enjoy all foods, moderately—without overindulging. Controlling the quantity of food you eat helps you maintain your weight—and, therefore, a healthier life-styles.

NUTRITION BASICS

Food provides both the energy and the materials needed to build and maintain all body cells. Nutrients are the nourishing substances found in food. Nutrition is the study of nutrients. Good nutrition is key to good health. Your body takes nutrients from the food you eat to physiologically exist.

So it's true—YOU ARE WHAT YOU EAT! What you put in your body effects how your body looks and feels. The healthier your food choices, the greater your chances for a healthy life-style.

A nutrition plan will work only if it's tailored specifically for you and the life-style you lead. THAT'S

WHY DIETS DON'T WORK! When you're on a diet, you're told what to eat, how much of it you can have, and when you can eat it.

DIETS ARE BORING AND RESTRICTIVE—ENOUGH SO THAT YOU'LL BREAK THEM EVERY TIME!

To personalize your nutrition plan, you need to assess your current nutrition, decide what small changes you're willing to make, and choose a variety of foods to meet your healthy life-style goals. Take an honest look at your current eating choices. Are you eating a variety of foods every day? Are many of the foods you eat high in fat? Do you eat foods with too much sugar and/or salt? Are you getting enough fiber? Do you consider the demands of your life-style when you decide what to eat?

Once you've assessed your own food intake, begin to make small changes in your eating habits. The smaller the change, the longer it will last—another reason why fad or crash diets just don't work! So don't vow never to eat a certain kind of food again. Instead, try one or two small changes in your eating habits per week.

Learn to make better choices with the foods you eat. Pick foods that are lower in fat and higher in fiber. Remember that you can eat anything you like—in moderation. The key is not to deprive yourself of foods you really like, but to work them into a better eating pattern.

MAKE SMALL CHANGES

You can change your eating habits and make them last if you start small. By making small changes, you're more likely to adopt these new habits and keep them over time. For example, if you eat a lot of salad, try using less dressing. I use regular dressing along with rice vinegar on most of my salads, limiting my regular dressing to only a teaspoon, dribbled slowly over my entire salad. This technique demonstrates how a little dressing can go a long way—with great taste. Instead of white bread, substitute whole wheat for greater nutritional value. If you find yourself eating every night at a fast food restaurant, try to change by fixing one dinner a week at home. These small changes add up to healthy results over time.

It's also helpful to eat a variety of foods daily. Your body needs more than 50 different nutrients every day from a wide variety of foods—complex carbohydrates, fruits and vegetables, proteins, dairy products and fats.

Remember to practice moderation in your eating habits as well. You don't need to practice any rigid diet or follow anything that suggests you eat too little—or too much. You'll find that by practicing moderation in your eating, you will eventually eat those foods that are best for your health and well-being.

LET'S TALK ABOUT FAT

What makes us like fat? Both animal and vegetable products contain fat—saturated (derived mostly from animals) and unsaturated (derived mostly from vegetables). Most fat really doesn't have a "taste" of its own—rather, it enhances food flavor.

The grease that cooks the french fries isn't what makes us crave fries. But the fat that the fries are cooked in does make them taste better. Fat dissolves the aromatic compounds of foods so that they affect our taste buds more easily. Thus, the grease enhances the taste of the fries. Fat is also hidden in many processed foods, such as crackers, quick breads, biscuits, muffins, cheese, doughnuts, pancakes, cookies and baked goods.

Reducing the amount of fat-laden foods we eat involves a reeducation of our taste buds. We need to restructure the foods we buy in the supermarket, how we prepare them, and what foods we order in a restaurant. We need to learn to substitute fatty substances with other flavorful items such as herbs and spices. We need to cook with less fat.

We don't want to eliminate fat altogether. This is virtually impossible anyway. Remember, food satisfaction is important to our healthy life-style, too. What we want to strive for is to gradually reduce our fat intake. Once again, moderation is the answer.

REDUCING YOUR FAT INTAKE

I advocate moderation, even with foods that are moderately high in fat. But if you really want to turn your body from a fat storehouse into a fat burnhouse, one way is to reduce your daily intake of fats.

If your goal is to lose fat, I recommend lowering your daily fat intake to a maximum of 30% of your daily calorie consumption. You can do this without sacrificing taste and food satisfaction, not to mention good nutrition.

It's impossible for me to tell you exactly how many grams of fat constitutes 30%—because 30% of my daily intake is different than your daily intake. You'll have to roughly figure out what 30% is by applying the fat formula on the following page.

If you really want to accelerate fat loss, try to limit your fat calories to 20% of your daily intake. I don't advocate this for long periods of time, because you lose food satisfaction. Let's face it, fat makes food taste better. When you sacrifice taste and satisfaction, you will eventually overeat. We should strive to lower our fat intake, not restrict it too severely. Anything between 20 and 30% is fine. Try, if you can, to keep fat under 30%.

Today, because labels have become more user-friendly, you won't need the following fat formula as often. As a further aid to calculating the fat in foods, food labels are now required to list the percentage of fat in a single serving.

FAT FORMULA

To determine the number of fat calories in food, remember that
I GRAM OF FAT = 9 CALORIES.

To convert fat grams to calories, simply multiply the grams X 9. Then, to determine the percentage of fat in that food, divide the fat calories by the total calories per serving.

Here's an example: 4 cups of popped microwave popcorn has
150 calories, 3 grams protein, 17 grams carbohydrates, 10 grams fat.

There are 10 grams of fat in one serving of popcorn.
10 grams X 9 calories per gram = 90 calories from fat.
90 Fat calories divided by 150 total calories = .6, or 60% fat.

At 60% fat, this popcorn has too much fat.
My recommendation would be to substitute air-popped popcorn with no added fat.

Any low-fat food you choose should have no more than 3 grams of fat per 100 calories.

FAT FACTS

Total fat is only part of the whole picture. There are two specific types of fat—saturated and unsaturated. Saturation refers to their chemical configuration.

SATURATED FATS
These generally come from animal sources and are solid at room temperature. Examples include:
- Butter, whole milk, cream, half & half
- Shortening
- Coconut oil, palm oil (although these come from plants)
- Higher fat proteins, such as certain cuts of beef and pork
- Eggs
- Baked goods and pastries that have a high concentration of cholesterol
- Chocolate

There is a strong relationship between the amount of saturated fats we consume and high blood cholesterol. What exactly is cholesterol? It's a fat-like substance that comes only from animal sources which, over time, builds up in the lining of our artery walls. As these fatty deposits build, the arteries shrink, causing high blood pressure and heart disease.

The good news is that by decreasing the amount of high cholesterol foods we eat, we can actually dissolve this build up gradually over time. In order to lower your blood cholesterol, you should try to reduce the amount of saturated fats in your diet.

UNSATURATED FATS

These come from plant sources and are liquid at room temperature. There are 2 types of unsaturated fats:

MONOUNSATURATED FATS:

- Olive oil
- Peanut oil
- Canola oil

POLYUNSATURATED FATS:

- Safflower oil
- Sunflower oil
- Cottonseed oil
- Corn oil
- Soybean oil
- Sesame oil

Although these fats are preferable to saturated fats, try to limit your amount of unsaturated fats as well.

Hydrogenated oils are unsaturated oils that have been processed to become solid at room temperature. Most margarines are made up of hydrogenated or partially hydrogenated oils. Most processed foods are loaded with these oils as well. Try to reduce the amount of hydrogenated oil foods you eat, especially reducing the amount of processed, packaged foods.

Choosing foods that are lower in fat is much easier than it used to be. Some low fat food is, frankly, inedible. But there are quite a number of foods that are low in fat and quite tasty. The challenge is to find food and recipes that give great taste and are lower in fat. My recipes included in this book have both.

Remember the price your body pays for high fat foods: heart disease, higher risk of certain cancers, sluggishness, less energy. Your body is like a luxury car—give it the best possible fuel! Cut down on fats!

HERE ARE SOME BASIC SUGGESTIONS TO LOWER THE FAT IN YOUR DIET.

CHOOSE:

- Low fat meats such as chicken, fish, and the leanest cuts of beef, pork and lamb.
- Low fat cooking methods—baking, broiling, grilling and sautéing in a nonstick pan.
- Oils and dressings that are lower in saturated fat.
- To use less fat—use smaller amounts of dressing on your salad, less butter or margarine on your bread or potato, etc.
- Herbs and spices to enhance food flavor.

EAT VERY SPARINGLY OR STAY AWAY FROM:

- High fat convenience and fast foods
- Whole milk, cheese
- High fat cuts of beef, pork and lamb
- Processed meats such as salami and bologna
- Baked goods

*Note: Some frozen prepared foods are lower in fat. However, these pricey foods are loaded with chemicals and preservatives. Watch your trade-offs.

EAT MORE FIBER

Fiber is GOOD! Fiber stimulates digestion, helps lower your risk of certain cancers and is lower in calories than other food groups. Fiber helps your body eliminate wastes more efficiently and easily. Grains, breads and cereals are good for you—as long as you don't smother them with fat!

Many people fear that increasing fiber in their diets will cause weight gain. But it's the FAT that we add to these foods that will add fat and pounds to our bodies.

To avoid bloating and general discomfort, add fiber gradually to your diet, and be sure to drink lots of water. I recommend six to eight (8-ounce) glasses of water per day.

Finally, don't go buy "fiber in a can." It's really easy to add fiber to your diet naturally. Try to eat a variety of whole grains, fresh fruits and vegetables every day.

HIGH FIBER CHOICES:
- Whole grains—brown rice, oatmeal, whole grain breads, pastas and cereals.
- Fresh fruits and veggies—straight from the garden or produce section. Frozen is okay. Canned fruits and vegetables should be your last choice.
- Legumes—kidney, garbanzo, and other dried beans.

SIMPLE WAYS TO INCREASE FIBER IN YOUR DIET.

- Include 2 servings of high-fiber food at every meal—make one a whole grain food and one a fruit or veggie.
- Eat a variety of fruits and veggies, especially those with seeds and skins. Try new ones! Experiment with dried beans, peas and legumes.
- Substitute whole wheat flour, oatmeal flour or oat bran for part or all of white flour when baking.
- Mix whole grains like oatmeal or oat bran into bread crumbs for cooking or breading. Choose whole grain pastas and brown rice over enriched pasta and white rice.
- Add high fiber garnishes such as bean sprouts, beets, shredded carrots, cabbage, cauliflower, broccoli, sunflower seeds, raisins, etc., to your salads.
- Choose vegetable and bean soups like minestrone, lentil and black bean over creamed soups.
- Choose cereals highest in fiber—read the labels! Good cereal sources of fiber have at least 4 to 5 grams per serving. Keep this in mind when reading cereal and bread labels.

BONE UP ON CALCIUM

Calcium is an essential mineral which helps build and maintain bones and teeth. Your body's hormones help keep a constant level of calcium in your blood. But you need to supply the calcium through foods rich in this mineral. If your diet is lacking in calcium, these hormones take some from your bones which causes them to weaken and be more susceptible to fractures.

Your body needs between 1000 to 1500 milligrams of calcium per day. Dairy products contain probably the highest amounts of calcium, but there are other foods that are calcium rich. Be sure the foods you select are low in fat.

GOOD SOURCES OF CALCIUM:

- Low and nonfat yogurt (frozen included)
- Sardines
- Part skim ricotta cheese
- Skim milk
- Low fat cheeses—Swiss, cheddar, cottage
- Oysters
- Salmon
- Collard and mustard greens
- Tofu, soybeans
- Dark green veggies—kale, broccoli, leaf and romaine lettuce, spinach

WATCH THE SUGAR

Sugar races into your bloodstream and gives you a "sugar high," a short-lived rush that ultimately leaves you more exhausted in the long run. Too much sugar can contribute to obesity, tooth decay, acne and diabetes.

Sugar has many names and comes in many forms, including: sucrose, glucose, dextrose, fructose, lactose, maple syrup, brown sugar, corn syrup, confectioners sugar, molasses, honey, etc. I like to use fructose because it contains fewer calories while delivering more sweetness than regular sugar. Fructose may also delay hunger. You can find it in most supermarkets.

In my estimation, artificial sweeteners pose an even greater threat to our health than eating foods high in sugar. Both saccharin and aspartame and their derivatives add unneeded chemicals and contaminants to your metabolism. Personally, I stay away from them.

So what's the answer? MODERATION! Sugar in moderation is fine in your diet—as long as you're not diabetic or sugar-restricted due to another health condition.

SIMPLE WAYS TO REDUCE SUGAR

- Go for fresh fruit or canned in its own juice, such as unsweetened pineapple.
- Develop a taste for bubbly drinks like sparkling mineral water, club soda or seltzer water. Add a lemon or lime for color and flavor.
- Gradually reduce the amount of sugar you use in coffee or tea, or sugar you add to unsweetened cereals.
- Substitute fructose for white table sugar.
- Buy jellies and jams made with fruit juices instead of sugar.
- MODERATION! If you have a taste for something sweet, take a bite or two. Or cut the portion in half.

HOLD THE SALT

Sodium is a mineral that occurs naturally in foods. It's needed in our bodies to help maintain our water balance. But Americans consume far more salt every day than our bodies require—largely because we eat so many processed, convenience foods, which contain huge quantities of sodium. Salt has been linked to high blood pressure because it brings extra water into your blood vessels which can cause pressure on the vessel walls.

The body needs about 1/10th of a teaspoon of sodium per day to maintain healthy function. Most people eat between 2 to 3 teaspoons daily! It's recommended that we consume no more than 1° teaspoons of salt per day. This will vary if you're on a sodium restricted diet.

SIMPLE WAYS TO REDUCE SODIUM

- Limit or avoid processed foods. This alone will cut your salt intake daily by at least one third. Eat fresh food!
- Stay away from fast food restaurants. Choose freshly prepared foods in restaurants.
- Select low sodium foods—unprocessed grains, fresh fruits and veggies, fresh meat, poultry, fish.
- Take the salt shaker off the table. Limit the salt you add to food while cooking.
- There are delicious herbs and spices that really wake up the flavor of food. Be adventurous! Try new ones!

ALCOHOL

Alcohol is one of the most widely abused substances in the United States today. It can lead to addiction, birth defects, impaired judgment, and can interact adversely with medications. There is no set level for safe drinking. We do know that having more than 2 drinks per day is directly related to high blood pressure.

Alcohol provides the body with more kilocalories than protein or carbohydrates. But where these nutrients provide other vitamins and minerals, alcohol does not. In fact, alcohol alters absorption and metabolism of all nutrients—even if you are eating properly, drinking alcohol will cause imbalances.

If you choose to drink, do so in moderation—keep it to 2 or less drinks per day. (Pregnant women should not drink alcohol in any amount.)

WRAP-UP

Good health is attainable by following good nutritional! You don't have to give up any food forever. By eating some foods occasionally and in moderation, you keep food satisfaction while practicing good nutrition. Fitting exercise into your life-style (Yes, you can! I'll show you how in Chapter Five) will help you feel better, think better, perform better. Eating well puts you on the road to a healthier life-style, and exercise is key to your total wellness. So here's to more energy, power, productivity, and better looks. Go for it! Good Luck!

Eating well requires that we know how to shop and what foods to buy at the supermarket. Once you learn what to shop for, this whole good nutrition/good health game gets so much easier. Turn the page to learn good shopping strategies.

Chapter Three

Shopping

LET'S GO SHOPPING:
A TRIP TO THE SUPERMARKET

Most people I meet hate the supermarket. I can't exactly tell you that I love food shopping, either, but I do know my way around the place, and I organize myself there just as I do in my kitchen.

Becoming a smart shopper will help you to become a wizard in your kitchen. The key—once again—is PLANNING! Planning sets you free—in the supermarket, in your kitchen, AND IN LIFE!

Smart shopping means healthy shopping, both for you and your wallet. Buying fresh food and using my recipes to prepare good food fast is not only better for you inside, but cheaper. Think about it—those frozen food entrées really add up.

SMART SHOPPING TIPS

Here's a list of shopping tips—your personal shopping blueprint—that will help you become a better shopper:

- Make a list! Going to the supermarket without a list is like going on a treasure hunt without a map—YOU'LL GET LOST AND NEVER FIND WHAT YOU'RE REALLY LOOKING FOR! Make a list when you're not hungry, take it with you and follow it! Write down grocery items as you need them until you're ready to go shopping. I call this my perennial shopping list. Keep your list tucked inside *Kitchen Express*, so you'll always know where it is.
- Browse through my recipes and incorporate ingredients you'll need into your shopping list.
- Ask your partner, spouse and/or family to help make the list.
- Organize your list by type of grocery item. This also speeds up your shopping time.
- Pick a good store—one that has fresh produce, grains, lean meats and poultry. AVOID CONVENIENCE STORES.
- Try not to shop when you're tired. If you're tired and have to shop, choose a smaller store, or one you know well. If you're really tired and still need groceries, take advantage of delivery services. Most of the supermarkets in my community offer delivery services. The delivery

charge is moderate, but the convenience of calling in your order and having someone else to do the shopping can be well worth it.

- Set a limit of how much you'll spend, or carry a set amount of money—so that you'll be less tempted to buy unnecessary items.

- If you're only picking up a few things, use a basket instead of a cart.

- Shop the perimeter of the supermarket—that's where the fresh food is: nutritious essentials like fruits and vegetables, lean meats and poultry, and low fat dairy products. The further you travel into the aisles, the more refined and processed the foods become. Avoid heavily processed foods and packaged mixes. Fresh is always best.

- Read the labels on food packages! Food labeling has come a long, long way. Labels now require listing the grams and percentages of fat, sodium, etc. Look at the labels on the food you're buying and try to choose those that are lower in fat. Look for the expiration dates and choose those packages with the most distant date.

- Remember, good nutrition doesn't have to be expensive. Lean cuts of beef, lamb, chicken, turkey, and pork usually cost less than the more expensive cuts. And remember that buying frozen entrées can really add up, too.

- Avoid those aisles in which you don't need anything. If you don't see that bag of chips, you're less likely to buy it.

- BEWARE OF IMPULSE ITEMS on the end of the aisles and at the checkout counters. Why do you think they put them there?
- Pick up a magazine while waiting in the checkout line, or review your grocery list. This will help "wandering eyes." Some grocery stores even have candy-free checkout lines—choose one of these!
- Put groceries away immediately when you arrive home. Don't leave food on the counters to tempt you.
- Congratulate yourself for shopping smartly! Affirm yourself with lots of positive self talk for adopting healthy shopping strategies! IF YOU'RE GOING TO BINGE ON ANYTHING, BINGE ON AFFIRMATIONS!
- AFFIRM! AFFIRM! AFFIRM!

FOOD LABELING

Food labels carry a wealth of information, but the terms can be confusing. Here's a quick rundown on definitions.

- **Lite or Light**: Food contains at least one-third fewer calories or has no more than half the fat of the original.

- **Free**: Food contains only an insignificant amount of a particular nutrient.
  - **Calorie Free**: Less than 5 calories per serving
  - **Fat Free**: Less than 0.5 g per serving
  - **Cholesterol Free**: Less than 2 mg per serving
  - **Sodium Free**: Less than 5 mg per serving
  - **Sugar Free**: Less than 0.5 mg of any type of sugar per serving
- **Lean**: Each 100-gram serving (3.5 ounces) contains less than 10 g of fat, 4 g of saturated fat, and 95 mg of cholesterol.
- **Extra Lean**: Each 100-gram serving contains less than 5 grams of fat, 2 grams of saturated fat and 95 mg of cholesterol.
- **Low**: You could eat the food frequently without exceeding the USDA dietary guidelines.
  - **Low Fat**: 3 grams or less per serving
  - **Low Saturated Fat**: 1 gram or less per serving
  - **Low Calorie**: 40 calories or less per serving
  - **Low Cholesterol**: Less than 20 mg per serving
  - **Low Sodium**: 140 mg or less per serving
  - **Very Low Sodium**: 35 mg or less per serving
- **Fewer**: Food contains 25 percent less of a nutrient or calories per serving than the standard product.

- **Good Source**: Food contains 10 to 19 percent of the daily value of a particular nutrient per serving.
- **More**: Food contains at least 10 percent more than 100 percent of the daily value for a particular vitamin, mineral or fiber per serving.

BASIC LOW FAT FOOD LIST

Here's a good, basic list of generic foods which are healthy and low fat. Choose those foods that you know and love—and then, try some new ones! Many of the ingredients that go into my recipes are listed here as well.

FRUITS AND VEGGIES
- All in liberal amounts except avocado, coconut and olives

MILK PRODUCTS
- Skim milk
- Any foods made from skim milk
- Cheese with less than 4 grams or less of fat per ounce
- Nonfat cottage cheese and sour cream
- Nonfat yogurt

BREADS AND CEREALS
- Plain breads and rolls—go for whole grain whenever possible
- Bagels (water bagels for the lowest fat)
- Nonfat pretzels, breadsticks and lowfat crackers
- Cereals—any brand with 3 grams or less of fat per serving
- Pasta
- Rice
- Starchy vegetables—potatoes, sweet potatoes, corn, peas, turnips, etc.
- Popcorn—no oil or butter added

MEAT, FISH, POULTRY, PROTEINS
Try to limit all meat servings to 3 ounces cooked weight per meal—about the size of a deck of cards.
- Skinless chicken and turkey
- Red meats—lean cuts, well trimmed
- Pork tenderloin
- Leg of lamb
- Most fish and shellfish
- Tuna packed in water (I prefer solid white)
- Canadian bacon trimmed

- Packaged sandwich meats with 2 grams or less of fat per ounce
- Dried beans, peas and legumes
- Egg whites

FATS AND OILS—ALL USED SPARINGLY
- Canola
- Safflower
- Corn
- Soybean
- Olive
- Stick margarines made from these oils
- Butter (sometimes better than margarines, used very sparingly)
- Low or no-fat mayonnaise
- Low or no-fat salad dressings (regular salad dressings used very sparingly)

CONDIMENTS, HERBS, SPICES, ETC.
- Mustards
- Ketchup—1 to 2 teaspoons per serving
- Vinegars—shop for flavored vinegars (I especially like rice and balsamic vinegar)
- Herbs and spices—fresh or dried (fresh is best)
- Bouillon, no-fat broths

DEE'S PICKS—BRAND NAME FOOD CHOICES

There are lots and lots of low and no-fat, brand name prepared foods on your supermarket shelves. Some are terrific. Some are... well, you might as well eat the box in which they're packaged.

I've tried many of these products. Listed in this section are my personal favorites. These foods are not only lower in fat or no-fat, they have an essential ingredient for anything that I put in my mouth—TASTE! I don't care if something has zero fat; if it lacks flavor, I won't eat it! Good flavor is critical.

Remember, these are my personal picks. You may find other brands that you like just as well or better. Feel free to experiment! But don't be too disappointed if the no-fat selection you make is also no-taste. Experiment. Don't count on any of these foods to taste great until you've tried them.

DAIRY
- Egg Beaters egg substitute
- Cool Whip Lite
- Land-O-Lakes Fat Free Sour Cream
- Land-O-Lakes Light Butter
- Breakstone Fat Free Sour Cream
- Breakstone Low Fat Cottage Cheeses
- Dannon Non-Fat Plain, Vanilla, Coffee and Lemon Yogurts

- Dannon Blended Fat-Free Yogurts—any flavor
- Jello Fat-Free Pudding Snacks
- I Can't Believe It's Yogurt Fat-Free and Sugar Free Toppings—Caramel and Fudge
- I Can't Believe It's Yogurt Non-Fat Frozen Yogurt—all flavors (only sold in these shops)
- Dairy Queen Non-Fat Vanilla Frozen Yogurt (only vanilla is non-fat)
- Kraft Light Naturals Shredded Low Moisture, Part Skim Mozzarella Cheese
- Sargento Light Shredded Cheeses—Mozzarella and Cheddar
- Ruggles Frozen Yogurt—any brand with 3 grams of fat or less per serving
- Philadelphia Free Cream Cheese
- Philadelphia Light Cream Cheese

BAKING, BAKED GOODS

- Betty Crocker Light cake, brownie and muffin mixes
- Pillsbury Lovin' Lites frostings
- Betty Crocker Fluffy White frosting mix—fat free
- Nabisco Fat-Free Newtons—all flavors
- Snackwells Cookies and Crackers—any flavor
- Healthy Greenfield Foods Fat-Free Brownies
- Mrs. Smiths Smart Style Desserts (I prefer apple)
- Angel Food Cake—any brand—fat free

- Entenmann's Fat Free Baked Goods—all flavors
- Hostess Lites—Twinkees and Cupcakes—I gram of fat per serving

OILS AND DRESSINGS
- Pam Cooking Sprays (I especially like Butter Flavor and Olive Oil)
- Le Pasce Extra Virgin Olive Oil
- Boyajian Garlic Olive Oil
- Consorzio Basil Olive Oil
- Fini Balsamic Vinegar
- Hellmann's Reduced Fat Mayonnaise
- Walden Farms Fat Free Caesar Salad Dressing
- Newman's Own Light Italian Salad Dressing
- T. Marzetti's Fat Free Peppercorn Ranch and Honey Dijon Salad Dressings

CANNED / JAR GOODS
- Motts Applesauces—any variety as long as it has no added sugar
- Bumblebee Solid White Tuna—water packed
- Polander All-Fruit Spreads—instead of jelly or jam
- Smucker's Simply Fruit Spreads
- St. Dalfour All Natural Fruit Conserves

MUNCHIES
- Harry's Non-Fat Sour Dough Pretzels
- Dutchie Honey Wheat Sour Dough Pretzels—fat free
- Snyder's Fat Free Pretzels
- Guiltless Gourmet No Oil Tortilla Chips and Bean Dips—all flavors
- Quaker Rice Cakes (I prefer Caramel Corn, but the White Cheddar and Apple Cinnamon flavors are good, too)

CEREALS
- Kelloggs Special K Cereal and Corn Flakes Cereal (my favorites, but choose any fat free cereals)
- Kelloggs Low Fat Granola

SAUCES AND CONDIMENTS
- French's Dijon Mustard with White Wine
- K.C. Masterpiece Original Barbeque Sauce
- Cowboy Caviar Fat Free Pasta Sauces
- Cowboy Caviar Vegetable Paté (served as a dip with no-oil tortilla chips)
- Marukan Seasoned Gourmet Rice Vinegar
- Angostura Low Sodium Soy and Teriyaki Sauces
- Contadina Italian Style Tomato Sauce

BREADS, ETC.
- Kelloggs Corn Flake Crumbs (for breading recipes)
- Orlando Ciabatta Bread
- Orlando Classic Italian Bread
- Maitre Jacques Dijon Mustard
- Boboli Pizza Crust Shells

SOUPS
- Progresso Pasta Soups and Low Fat Soups—1 gram or less of fat per serving
- Tabatchnick Frozen Low Fat Soups—less than 1 gram/serving

MEATS
- La Belle Rouge Free Range Chicken

PASTAS AND RICE
- dei Martelli—all brands (can be found at Williams Sonoma)
- Williams Sonoma California Seven Rice Blend (Williams Sonoma)

Appetizers & More .... page 53

Salads .... page 65

Soups, Vegetables & Pasta .... page 69

Poultry, Meat & Seafood .... page 99

Desserts .... page 129

Chapter Four

Dee's Kitchen Express Recipes

I'm so proud to present these recipes, for they are truly the keys to making good food fast! Most of these recipes are my own tried-n-true favorites. Some have been graciously given to me by friends and clients. All of them have been tested in my own kitchen.

Each recipe has been analyzed for calories, fat, carbohydrates, protein, etc., by a licensed dietitian—so that you'll know exactly what's in the food you're preparing. Many of them are low-fat; some have a moderate amount of fat. Please refer to the fat formula and your daily fat allowance in Chapter Three, so that you can decide which recipe you'll try for a particular meal.

Most of these recipes have a moderate amount of sodium. If you're on a sodium restricted diet, all you have to do is to eliminate any salt that's listed in the recipe ingredients. Also, substitute low-salt items, such as low-sodium tomato sauce/pasta/soup for the ingredients listed.

Try one or try 'em all! I think you'll find any of them easy to prepare and a snap to store and reheat for future meals. Each recipe is a healthy alternative to prepared or fast foods—and loaded with an essential ingredient—**flavor**! Happy cooking and bon appetite!

Appetizers & More

HORSY SHRIMP DIP

Serve this dip with lots of warmth and good conversation. Perfect for get-togethers, the creamy combination of horseradish, shrimp and spinach is unbeatable. And if eaten in moderation, you have a great low fat appetizer.

Makes 2¾ cups (22 servings).

Appearance Result

A colorful, festive dip.

Nutritional Analysis

Per Serving (2 tablespoons): 77.3 Calories; 5.85 g fat; 3.4 g Sat. Fat; 30.8 g Cholesterol; 174 mg Sodium; 1.5 g Carbohydrates; .25 Fiber; 4 g Sugar; 4.3 g Protein

Dee's Suggestions

Serve with crackers, cocktail bread or raw veggies—and good friends.

HORSY SHRIMP DIP

- 1 (8-ounce) package regular Philadelphia Cream Cheese
- 1 (8-ounce) package light Philadelphia Cream Cheese
- 1/3 cup white horseradish (jar)
- 1/4 teaspoon pepper
- 1/2 teaspoon salt
- 1/4 cup minced scallions
- 1/4 cup dry parsley
- 1 box frozen spinach, cooked and drained (optional)
- 1 (6-ounce) can tiny shrimp, rinsed and drained

Let cream cheese soften approximately 1 hour until it reaches room temperature. Add all ingredients except shrimp and mix well with wooden spoon. Add shrimp and mix.

GARLIC-Y WHITE BEAN SPREAD

Another winner of an appetizer—Zesty with garlic and low in fat. Vegetarians will love it.

Makes one cup (8 servings).

Appearance Result

A white creamy spread.

Nutritional Analysis

Per Serving (2 tablespoons): 142 Calories; 2.4 g Fat; .15 g Sat. Fat; 0 g Cholesterol; 279 mg Sodium; 27 g Carbohydrates; 6 g Fiber; 0 g Sugar; 10.1 g Protein

Dee's Suggestions

Refrigerate and serve cold with cut-up veggies or low fat crackers.

★

GARLIC-Y WHITE BEAN SPREAD

2 (19-ounce) cans white beans
¼ teaspoon salt
6 tablespoons fresh crushed garlic
2 teaspoons olive oil
2 tablespoons dry parsley (or fresh flat Italian parsley)

Wash and drain beans in colander. Add beans to remaining ingredients and blend in food processor or blender until a smooth paste, or mash with potato masher to a mashed-potato consistency.

GAMEKEEPER'S COLD SHRIMP APPETIZER WITH FRUIT

Feel like showing off? This impressive appetizer is for you. It looks marvelous and the unique combination of ingredients will tantalize all your taste buds.

Makes 4 servings.

Nutritional Analysis

Per serving (does not include dressing): 220 Calories; 5.7 g Fat; 0.6 g Sat. Fat; 87 mg Cholesterol; 210 mg Sodium; 31 g Carbohydrates; 4.8 g Fiber; 24 g Sugar; 15 g Protein

Dee's Suggestions

A great beginning to any meal.

Appetizers & More • 58

GAMEKEEPER'S COLD SHRIMP APPETIZER WITH FRUIT

8 ounces cooked shrimp
4 ounces diced red apple
4 ounces diced pear
6 ounces seedless red grapes, halved
2 ounces diced red onion
2 ounces raisins
4 teaspoons chopped fresh dill (or 1 teaspoon dried dill weed)
1 ounce roasted walnuts
Balsamic vinaigrette dressing to your liking
Spinach leaves

Chill four plates. Mix together all the ingredients except the spinach, making sure the diced apple and pear is ripe and not discolored. Toss the spinach with the rest of the ingredients and serve on the plates.

GARNET CRANBERRY RELISH

A magnificent recipe that's a superb companion, worthy of any entrée. It's good looking, great tasting, and fat and chemical free. This relish can also be used in desserts—read on!

Appearance Result
Deep garnet red color, chunky.

Nutritional Analysis
Per Serving (1 ounce): 35 Calories; 0g Fat, Sat Fat, and Cholesterol; 2 mg Sodium; 9 g Carbohydrates; 0 g Fiber; 8 g Sugar; 0 g protein.

Dee's Suggestions
This recipe can be stored in your refrigerator. When transferring into storage containers, you may want to drain off some of the juice, so that the relish isn't runny but still very moist. This makes a very large quantity in a short amount of cooking time. It will freeze beautifully—so you have the joy of eating cranberries in June! It is also incredible served half frozen over non-fat frozen vanilla yogurt. A relish that can transform itself into a dessert—YUM!

GARNET CRANBERRY RELISH

3 (20-ounce) cans unsweetened crushed pineapple
6 cups water
8 cups sugar
6 cups fresh cranberries (6 bags)
3 small (3-ounce) boxes lemon Jell-O

Drain and save juice from the pineapple. In a large, 4-quart pot, add water, sugar and drained pineapple juice. Bring to a boil. Wash and drain cranberries; add to boiling mixture. Cook about 10 minutes until cranberries have burst. Remove from heat. Mix lemon Jell-O with a little water to moisten; add to cranberry mixture. Add drained, unsweetened crushed pineapple. Refrigerate or freeze until ready to serve with entrées or on desserts.

DEE'S MAGIC MIX

"Gee, Toto, I don't think we're in Kansas anymore!" Only Dee's Magic Mix will transform your recipes from plain, boring food into culinary delights—straight from the land of Oz!

Makes 9 ounces.

Appearance Result
Dried herb mixture.

Nutritional Analysis
Per (1-ounce) serving (2 tablespoons): 31 Calories; 0.9 g Fat; 0 g Sat. Fat; 0 g Cholesterol; 6.7 mg Sodium; 6.3 g Carbohydrates; 0 g Fiber; 0 g Sugar; 1.6 g Protein

Dee's Suggestions
I use Dee's Magic Mix on meat, poultry and fish. Sprinkle liberally. It stores indefinitely in a airtight plastic container. Keep on hand to enhance food flavor and send your taste buds "Over the Rainbow."

Appetizers & More • 62

DEE'S MAGIC MIX

6 tablespoons oregano
6 tablespoons sweet basil
2 tablespoons garlic powder
2 tablespoons tarragon
3 tablespoons parsley flakes
4 tablespoons paprika
1 teaspoon black pepper

Mix all ingredients together, and use generously on all your favorite recipes.

Salads

SALADS—QUICK, EASY, NUTRITIOUS EATING (A BUSY PERSON'S DREAM FOOD)

Salads have so many virtues—"lettuce" (oh, brother!) count the ways!

- Heathly, super nutritious
- Created in minutes
- Filling
- Cool, crispy and crunchy
- Cleansing to your palate
- Provide maximum taste satisfaction
- With creativity, they'll never bore you

I'm leaving it up to you to build your own salad. In this section, I make suggestions and you take it from there. Because there are so many variations of salads, depending upon what YOU like, I haven't included nutritional analysis. Keep in mind that most veggies have no fat—it's what you put on your salad that does.

When building your salad, remember—the darker the greens, the more nutritious the dish. Just one cup of spinach, chard, collard, mustards, or watercress provides 100% of the USRDA for Vitamin A—and only 10 calories.

Dee's secret to lettuce longevity: "Spinning and Storing," using a salad spinner and an airtight container! The salad spinner is the best salad investment you can make in your kitchen. When using the spinner, wash your greens thoroughly, place them in the spinner basket, place the basket inside the outer spinner bowl, cover with the lid and SPIN! The spinning process extracts enough of the water from the greens, leaving you with lettuce that's superclean and marvelously crisp. Then, store the greens in an airtight container in your refrigerator. This way, the greens keep for a week to 10 days—and you'll have the convenience of building a terrific, healthy salad in minutes! You'll never again have to eat wilted, watery greens if you practice "spinning and storing."

Be as creative as you like when building your salad. Salad making should be fun and should take only minutes. Without special topping, they play second fiddle well to any entrée you're serving. As a main, attraction, they're guaranteed to satisfy. Have a ball! Oops—I mean, have a bowl!

SALAD WIZARDRY—HOW TO BUILD A BETTER SALAD

1 Begin with your favorite **salad greens...**

2 Add your favorite **veggies.**

I love:

- red, sweet bell pepper
- green bell pepper
- yellow bell pepper
- cucumbers
- shredded carrots
- red cabbage
- tiny sweet peas (frozen, defrosted)
- onions
- tomatoes
- broccoli flowerets
- cauliflower

3 Add **toppings***—any leftovers you have in your refrigerator can be added to the top of your salad. For example:

- from my Rump Roast recipe, cut leftover slices in strips
- grilled chicken, cut in strips
- water-packed tuna, drained and flaked over greens. I strongly recommend white albacore water-packed tuna for best flavor.
- canned salmon, drained well and flaked over greens
- cooked shrimp—for a very special topping

*If you're watching your fats, 3 to 4-ounce portions per person should be your rule of thumb.

4 **Dressing**—Dress your salad lightly. Drowning a wonderful, fresh salad with a heavy, oil-based dressing is a BIG MISTAKE! This turns a low-to-moderate-fat salad into a high-fat meal. I start with a base of rice vinegar sprinkled over my salad, then add 1 to 2 tablespoons of my favorite dressing.

Salads • 68

Soups, Vegetables, & Pasta

MARSHA'S CHICKEN CHILI

My editor, Marsha, makes this recipe. Boy, is this great chili—aromatic and full of flavor—tantalizing to your taste buds, and very, very satisfying. And, what's more, it's easy to prepare. Enjoy it anytime, but especially on a frosty winter day—it will warm you all over.

Makes over one gallon.

Appearance Result
Sunny burnt orange in color, studded with yellow and green.

Nutritional Analysis
Per (1-cup) serving: 229 Calories; 6 g Fat; 0 g Sat. Fat; 62 mg Cholesterol; 660 mg Sodium; 28 g Carbohydrates; 4 g Sugar; 17 g Protein.

Dee's Suggestions
This chili is so tasty—it's my very favorite chili recipe. Preparation time takes about 20 minutes. While it's cooking (1 hour), you're free to do other things around the house. The chili keeps in the fridge for over a week and freezes beautifully. It actually tastes better after it's been frozen and thawed, because the spices mingle longer with the rest of the ingredients. This one's a real winner!

MARSHA'S CHICKEN CHILI

2 tablespoons olive oil
2 cups chopped onion
1 tablespoon chopped garlic
2 pounds ground chicken
2 teaspoons curry powder
2 teaspoons black pepper
¼ teaspoon cayenne*
2 teaspoons ground coriander
1 tablespoon cumin
1 banana pepper, chopped in small pieces
½ teaspoon cinnamon
Pinch of nutmeg
1 (16-ounce) can tomato soup
1 can water
1 (28-ounce) can crushed tomatoes
1 (6-ounce) can tomato paste
6 ounces frozen corn
1 tablespoon salt
1 teaspoon sugar
2 (14-ounce) cans pinto beans—1 can pureéd in blender or food processor, 1 can whole and drained
2 tablespoons dried chives

* Increase for spicier chili.

In a large stock pot, heat olive oil on medium heat until hot. Add chopped onion and cook until transparent. Add garlic and cook until soft. Add the ground chicken and cook about 12 minutes until chicken is cooked through. Add all the remaining ingredients except the dried chives, including the pinto beans, and stir thoroughly until well blended. Reduce heat to low and simmer, stirring occasionally for 1 hour. Remove from heat, add dried chives and stir. Serve immediately.

HEARTY-HEARTY VEGETABLE BEEF SOUP

Oh, the weather outside may be frightful, but the smells from your kitchen are delightful! So what if you've no place to go—let it snow, let it snow! You've got this soup to keep you warm!

Makes 4 servings.

Appearance Result

Classic vegetable beef soup.

Nutritional Analysis

Per Serving: 401 Calories; 13.8 g Fat; 3.2 g Sat. Fat; 81 g Cholesterol; 1,018 mg Sodium; 36.4 g Carbohydrates; 3.9 g Fiber; 37.25 g Sugar; 34.2 g Protein

Dee's Suggestions

Since this soup is so hearty and flavorful, it is a meal in itself. Double (or triple!!) the recipe and freeze in various size containers. Caution—if you make it on Sunday, you'll still be craving it the following Friday. Keeps in the refrigerator for one week.

Soups, Vegetables & Pasta • 72

HEARTY-HEARTY VEGETABLE BEEF SOUP

1 pound chuck roast, stew meat, or other inexpensive cut of beef
5 cups water
2 tablespoons oil
1 cup chopped onion
3 small potatoes, peeled and diced
1 (9-ounce) package frozen mixed vegetables
1 (14½-ounce) can no-salt-added stewed tomatoes
2 tablespoons dry sweet basil
1 teaspoon salt
1 teaspoon black pepper
1 teaspoon Lawry's seasoning salt

Put beef in large pot with water. Bring to a boil, lower heat and simmer 1 hour. Remove meat, dice and return to pot. Heat oil in pan and sauté onions for 3 minutes. Mix in potatoes, frozen veggies, stewed tomatoes and seasonings; remove form heat and add to beef soup and simmer 1 more hour. Adjust seasonings as needed.

SHRIMP CREOLE

This is one of my favorite seafood recipes (given to me by my client, Terri Applegate)—New Orleans-style shrimp creole, modified to be very low in fat and so very tasty! If you really crave hot-n-spicy food, you can make this even hotter by adding more cayenne pepper. Y'all try this one for sure!

Makes six servings.

Appearance Result

Very colorful—like New Orleans!

Nutritional Analysis

Per Serving (1 cup): 150 Calories; 1 g Fat; 0 g Sat. Fat, 95 mg Cholesterol; 910 mg Sodium; 22 g Carbohydrates 1 g Fiber, 3 g Sugar; 15 g Protein. This recipe is high in sodium. To reduce the sodium, eliminate the salt from the recipe and use no-salt bouillon.

Dee's Suggestions

This recipe is a snap to make—about 20 minutes preparation time. It's so tasty and looks beautiful on the plate! It also freezes very well. In fact, I recommend freezing over refrigerator storage for this one because the shrimp retains its flavor better in the freezer.

SHRIMP CREOLE

- 1 medium onion
- 1 green pepper
- 1 red pepper
- 2 cloves garlic
- 2 tablespoons light butter (or margarine)
- 1 teaspoon salt
- 1 teaspoon black pepper
- 1½ teaspoons paprika
- 1 teaspoon cayenne pepper*
- 2 (16½-ounce) cans stewed tomatoes, undrained
- 2 teaspoons chicken bouillon granules
- 1 teaspoon sugar
- 1½ teaspoons dried thyme
- 1½ teaspoons dried basil
- 2 tablespoons cornstarch
- ¼ cup water
- 1 pound cooked fresh shrimp (medium size)
- Snipped parsley for garnish

Chop onion and green and red peppers. Mince garlic. In a large saucepan or Dutch oven, combine the onion, garlic and peppers in the butter. Add salt, pepper, paprika and cayenne pepper. Sauté over medium heat until soft.

Stir into the pot the undrained tomatoes, bouillon granules, sugar, thyme and basil. Simmer uncovered for about 10 minutes.

In a small bowl, combine cornstarch and water and mix together so there are no lumps. Stir into the tomato mixture in the pot and cook 3 to 4 minutes. Add the shrimp and simmer for another 3 to 4 minutes, until the shrimp is heated through. Be sure not to overcook the shrimp.

Serve over hot steamed rice and garnish with parsley.

*For a milder recipe, use half a teaspoon, or omit entirely.

VEGETABLE LASAGNA

Colorful, low in fat, easy to prepare and terrific! When you have a taste for Italian, this is it!

Makes 15 servings.

Appearance Result

Colorful, layered, sunny and Italian! Golden brown mozzarella on top, red-saucy good!

Nutritional Analysis

Per (10-ounce) Serving: 302 Calories; 12 g Fat; 5 g Sat. Fat; 50 mg Cholesterol; 887 mg Sodium; 28 g Carbohydrates; 2 g Fiber; 2 g Sugar; 20 g Protein

Dee's Suggestions

My friend, Mary Beth Thomas, shared this recipe with me, and it's become a mainstay. Serve this great, low-fat Italian classic with a side salad and ciabatta bread—hearty and delicious. I slice the lasagne into 15 squares and freeze them individually, so that I can pull single portions out of the freezer and reheat. What could be better or faster!

VEGETABLE LASAGNA

1 pound Lasagna noodles
2 pounds low-fat skim ricotta cheese
1 tablespoon oregano
1 tablespoon dried basil
1 teaspoon salt
½ teaspoon pepper
½ cup grated Parmesan cheese
½ cup Egg Beaters
2 tablespoons parsley flakes
1 green pepper
1 red pepper
1 small yellow squash
1 small zucchini
1 cup broccoli flowerets
1½ cups onions, coarsely chopped
2 cloves fresh garlic, minced
2 (25-ounce) jars low-fat spaghetti sauce
12 ounces low-fat mozzarella (4 grams fat or less per serving)

Preheat oven to 375 degrees. Boil 6 quarts of water in a large stock pot. Cook the lasagne noodles in the boiling water for 10 minutes while preparing the rest of the recipe. Drain in a colander.

Mix together ricotta, spices, parmesan, Egg Beaters, and parsley flakes, and set aside.

Cut green and red peppers into 1-inch squares. Slice yellow squash and zucchini thinly. Cut broccoli into small pieces. Sauté with onions and garlic in large, nonstick pan lightly coated with cooking spray until veggies are crispy tender, about five to eight minutes.

In a 10 X 15-inch pan, begin with a thin layer of sauce in the bottom; then layer ⅓ of the cooked noodles, ½ of the cheese mixture, ½ of the veggies, ⅓ of the spaghetti sauce, and ⅓ of the grated mozzarella. Repeat layers.

Bake for 45 minutes in preheated 375 degree oven. Let set for 10 minutes before slicing. Slice into 15 equal portions.

VERSATILE BASIL PASTA SAUCE (MEATLESS)

This sauce is my favorite—versatile, low in fat and delicious. It will win over your tastebuds—explodes with nutrition, AND has only 1 gram of fat per serving—AMAZING! The fresh basil really makes it taste special. Fresh basil can be found in small packages in the produce section of your supermarket.

Makes 4 quarts cooked sauce.

Appearance Result

Thick, red, substantive, chunky but light in taste. Not soupy; like sauce from a jar.

Freezer Instructions

This sauce can be stored in your refrigerator for up to 10 days. It freezes beautifully for up to four months.

Nutritional Analysis

Per (4-ounce) Serving: 49 Calories; 1 g Fat; 0 g Sat. Fat; 0 mg Cholesterol; 225 mg Sodium; 8 g Carbohydrates; 0 g Fiber; 3 g Sugars; 1 g Protein.

Dee's Suggestions

This is a perfect recipe to make on Saturday or Sunday morning or afternoon when you are home. It takes only 20 minutes to prepare the ingredients for cooking. During cooking time, you're free to do other things around the house. This recipe makes lots of sauce, great for freezing and reheating anytime you have a taste for pasta. This is also the base sauce for my ratatouille recipe.

Ladle this sauce over two or more different pastas for a gourmet look and taste. I like to serve it in individual pasta bowls with grated Parmesan over top.

Add versatility by adding extras to the sauce—sautéed shrimp, grilled chicken, or anything your taste desires.

Soups, Vegetables & Pasta • 78

VERSATILE BASIL PASTA SAUCE (MEATLESS)

6 large onions

9 cloves crushed garlic, divided

5 bags of fresh basil—approximately 2 cups

2 bunches flat-leaf parsley (not curly)—approximately 1¼ cups

1 cup cooked fresh spinach

2 cups fresh green beans

6 (28-ounce) cans Italian style plum tomatoes, peeled, with basil added

2 cups dry red wine (whatever you have on hand, as long as it's dry)

1½ teaspoons coarsely ground pepper

5 tablespoons sugar or to taste

6 tablespoons olive oil

Slice the onions in rounds—whole or half. In a large, nonstick skillet, slowly sauté the onions with 2 cloves of the crushed garlic until onions are soft and translucent.

Wash the basil and parsley, drain and pat dry with a paper towel.

Remove the stems from the spinach and wash thoroughly in a salad spinner or colander. Cook with a little water in a small saucepan on low heat for about 10 minutes until tender. After cooking, drain the spinach thoroughly and put aside.

Wash the green beans, cut off the ends and put in boiling water about 3 minutes; cook al dente (crispy tender). Rinse in cold water, drain and put aside.

In a 4-quart Dutch oven or stockpot, add canned tomatoes, breaking them slightly with a spoon. Add red wine, the remaining crushed garlic, ground pepper, sugar, olive oil, sautéed onions, basil, parsley, cooked spinach and green beans. Cook on low heat for about 4 hours.

DEE'S RATATOUILLE

This dish was borne out of my infamous pasta sauce—another delectable variation. A super-nutritious side dish, or, for my vegetarian friends, a great main dish. Easy, easy easy!

Makes about 4 (8-ounce) servings.

Appearance Result
Rust-red-sauce dish loaded with colorful yellow and green.

Nutritional Analysis
Per (8-ounce) serving: 121 Calories; 2 g Fat; 0 g Sat. Fat; 0 mg Cholesterol; 225 mg Sodium; 23 g Carbohydrates; 2 g Fiber; 9 g Sugar; 3 g Protein

Dee's Suggestions
I like to serve this as a side dish in individual shallow bowls with a big slice of hot bread (no butter). Like my pasta sauce, this Ratatouille has storage and freezer power.

DEE'S RATATOUILLE

2 medium zucchini
2 medium yellow squash
2½ cups Dee's Versatile Basil Pasta Sauce

Wash both squash well and cut into quarter-inch round slices. Cook in one cup of the pasta sauce for about 15 minutes, until the slices are soft. Add the remaining 1½ cups sauce (or more, if additional liquid is required) and heat through. Serve.

20-MINUTE VEGETARIAN EGGPLANT TAPINADE

Want to impress? Serve this dish. Its versatility is endless; its taste is extraordinary. You'll make it again and again.

Makes six (4-ounce) servings.

Appearance Result

Chunky, thick, tomato red in color.

Nutritional Analysis

Per (4-ounce) Serving: 88.3 Calories; 3.0 g Fat; 0.46 g Sat. Fat: 0 g Cholesterol; 492.8 mg Sodium; 9.1 g Carbohydrates; 1.5 g Fiber; 3.3 g Sugar; 2.4 g Protein

Dee's Suggestions

This versatile recipe can be served hot as a side dish or as a main dish over angel hair pasta or rice. My favorite is to serve it cold, accompanied with thin slices of Italian bread or pita.

20-MINUTE VEGETARIAN EGGPLANT TAPINADE

1 tablespoon olive oil
1 large fresh eggplant, chopped
2 green zucchini, chopped
1 medium onion, chopped
4 cloves garlic, chopped
1 (15-ounce) can tomato sauce
1 teaspoon sweet basil
1 teaspoon dry oregano
¼ cup whole pitted black olives*

*Omit and decrease your fat to 2.5 grams per serving.

Heat olive oil. Add eggplant, zucchini, onion and garlic and sauté until soft, approximately 10 minutes. Add tomato sauce, herbs, and olives; cover and simmer 10 more minutes.

MILLI-G'S VEGETABLE CAKES

A great low-fat choice for a delicious side dish or an exciting appetizer. A real crowd pleaser! Looks good and fun to eat.

Makes about 10 cakes.

Nutritional Analysis

Per serving (1 cake): 70 Calories; 2 g Fat; 1 g Sat. Fat; 4 mg Cholesterol; 142 mg Sodium; 8 g Carbohydrates; 2 g Fiber; 2 g Sugar; 6 g Protein

Dee's Suggestions

This one's simple, put them on a plate, serve, and enjoy the complements.

MILLI-G'S VEGETABLE CAKES

1 medium zucchini
2 carrots
1 green pepper
1 bunch green onions
2 cloves garlic, minced
8 ounces egg whites or Egg Beaters
½ cup whole wheat or all purpose flour
½ cup Parmesan cheese
½ tablespoon dill weed
4 dashes tabasco sauce
Salt and pepper to taste

Preheat oven to 350 degrees. Dice the first five ingredients and place in a bowl. Add the egg whites or Egg Beaters and flour; mix well. Add the Parmesan cheese, dill, tabasco sauce, salt and pepper, mixing well again. Spray a cookie sheet with nonstick cooking oil. Scoop the batter into tennis ball-sized balls, place evenly on cookie sheet and flatten slightly into cakes. Lightly spray tops of the cakes with cooking spray and bake 30 minutes.

SKILLET POTATOES AND VEGETABLES

A quick, hearty dish, bursting with flavor. This can be used as the main attraction, or as a side dish. Bonus: an excellent source of potassium and Vitamin C. As a side dish, this serves five people easily.

Appearance Result
Colorful.

Nutritional Analysis
Per (8-ounce) Serving: 300 Calories; 4 g Fat; 0 g Sat. Fat; 0 g Cholesterol; 76 mg Sodium; 60 g Carbohydrates; 10 g Fiber; 7 g Sugars; 9 g Protein.

Dee's Suggestions
Use this hearty, nutritious dish when first made as a side dish to an entrée. It stores well in your refrigerator for a week to ten days. I often use it as a main dish—great for lunch! Have fun with this one!

SKILLET POTATOES AND VEGETABLES

5 medium to large potatoes
2 cups fresh broccoli, cut into small pieces
1 tablespoon olive oil
1 cup frozen peas, defrosted
1 red bell pepper, seeded and diced
2 cloves crushed garlic
2 bunches green onions, chopped
1 teaspoon dried sweet basil
Salt, black pepper and red pepper to taste*

*Use sparingly if you don't like your food too spicy.

Slice unpeeled potatoes into 1-inch cubes. Boil 8 minutes. Add broccoli into boiling potatoes and cook for another 4 to 5 minutes, until potatoes are tender. Drain. Heat olive oil in deep skillet (nonstick if available). Add drained potatoes, broccoli and remaining ingredients. Sauté until all ingredients are heated through—about 7 minutes.

FAT FREE GARLIC MASHED POTATOES

This recipe will really make you look good! It's creamy, full of flavor, and will make any meal you serve special. Yes, a great potato dish with all the fat removed.

Makes six (8-ounce) servings.

Appearance Result

Fluffy white and creamy.

Nutritional Analysis

Per (8-ounce) Serving: 238 Calories; 0 g Fat; 0 Sat. Fat; 1 mg Cholesterol; 37 mg Sodium; 54 g Carbohydrates; 5 g Fiber; 5 g Sugars; 6 g Protein.

Dee's Suggestions

This is a great side dish, long on satisfaction—real tummy food! It stores well in your refrigerator for about a week, and in the microwave in a snap. If you're in the mood for potato pancakes, form pancakes with the mixture, sprinkle with paprika and sauté in a nonstick skillet with cooking spray or a little olive oil, and you have delicious, low-fat potato pancakes like magic!

Soups, Vegetables & Pasta • 88

FAT FREE GARLIC MASHED POTATOES

5 garlic cloves
6 large Idaho potatoes with skin
1 cup skim milk, heated*
Salt and pepper to taste

*You may not need a full cup of skim milk—just add enough so that the potatoes are creamy.

In a medium size saucepan, boil water with the 5 cloves of garlic. While the water comes to a boil, scrub the potatoes well with a vegetable brush. Leave the skin on for the fullest nutritional benefit. Cut the potatoes into medium-size pieces, about 2-inch cubes. Put into the boiling water and cook until soft, about 12 minutes. Drain in colander, leaving the garlic cloves in the potatoes.

Mash the potatoes with masher until completely smooth. Gradually pour in heated skim milk until smooth and creamy. Season with salt and pepper.

NO-FAT WHIPPED SPINACH POTATOES

I guarantee this recipe will turn a confirmed spinach-hater into a spinach-lover forever! This is a real family favorite—and my friends love it! The perfect marriage of taste and texture, color and nutrients. You'll love it, too—try it!

Makes six servings.

Appearance Result

Smooth with spinach green swirls.

Nutritional Analysis

Per Serving (11 ounces): 259 Calories; 0 g Fat; 0 g Sat. Fat; 1 mg Cholesterol; 102 mg Sodium; 58 g Carbohydrates; 7 g Fiber; 5 g Sugars; 9 g Protein.

Dee's Suggestions

This is a wonderful, nutritious recipe. I can't think of a better way to eat spinach. It stores in your refrigerator for about a week. Reheat for many more great meals. The leftover spinach potatoes, warmed in the microwave, can also be put onto a small broiling pan and sprinkled with paprika, then place under the broiler until brown. Looks crispy outside, fluffy and tender inside.

NO-FAT WHIPPED SPINACH POTATOES

5 garlic cloves
6 large Idaho potatoes with skin
1 large package fresh spinach (approximately 1 pound) or 1 (10-ounce) box frozen spinach (pieces, not whole leaves)*
1 cup skim milk, heated
1 tablespoon dried sweet basil
Salt and pepper to taste

*Fresh spinach is preferred.

In a medium-size saucepan, boil water with the 5 cloves of garlic. While the water comes to a boil, scrub the potatoes well with a vegetable brush. Leave the skin on for the fullest nutritional benefit. Cut the potatoes into medium-size pieces, about 2-inch cubes. Put into the boiling water and cook until soft, about 12 minutes. Drain in colander, leaving the garlic cloves in the potatoes.

While potatoes are boiling, wash and drain spinach, if using fresh. Remove stems and place in medium saucepan. Add ° cup water and cook until tender, about 5 to 7 minutes. Drain thoroughly; make sure to press all the liquid out of the spinach or it will make the potatoes runny. (If using frozen spinach, follow package directions for cooking. Drain thoroughly.)

Mash the potatoes with masher until completely smooth. Gradually pour in heated skim milk until smooth and creamy. (You may not need a full cup of skim milk. Just add enough until creamy.)

Be sure the spinach is well drained—no liquid—and fold into the potatoes, along with the basil. Salt and pepper to taste.

HERBED BAKED SWEET POTATOES

Sweet potatoes other than at Thanksgiving? Try these; they'll sweeten your day with energy and nutritional value—and you won't believe the taste! Sweet potatoes are loaded with vitamins, especially Vitamin A, and contain more calcium, iron, potassium and niacin than regular white potatoes. Yams can also be used, but they taste slightly different, a bit less sweet. Try to find sweet potatoes, if possible. This recipe is a wonderful accompaniment to most any entrée. Or eat them solo. They're wonderfully filling.

Serves 4 as a side dish.

Appearance Result

Dark brown and crusty on the outside, soft and honey-gold on the inside.

Nutritional Analysis

Per Serving (one sweet potato quarter): 118 Calories; 4 g Fat; 0 g Sat. Fat; 0 g Cholesterol; 9 mg Sodium; 21 g Carbohydrates; 2 g Fiber; 9 g Sugar; 2 g Protein.

Dee's Suggestions

Remember, this sweet potato recipe will stay fresh, tightly wrapped, in your refrigerator for up to 2 weeks.

HERBED BAKED SWEET POTATOES

1 large sweet potato
1 tablespoon olive oil
1 tablespoon sweet basil
1 tablespoon paprika
1 tablespoon oregano
1 teaspoon garlic powder
1 teaspoon tarragon
1 teaspoon celery salt
1 teaspoon dried parsley flakes

Preheat oven to 400 degrees. Scrub the sweet potato well and cut into quarters. In a mid-sized bowl, mix well with large spoon the olive oil and all the dry ingredients. With a pastry brush, cover each sweet potato quarter with the olive oil-herb mixture, covering each quarter well. Place in a small baking pan lined with foil, and bake. Test by inserting a fork after 30 minutes—the potato should be soft. If not, allow to cook a bit more.

LOW-FAT PASTA SENSATION

This satisfying dish, once made (20 minutes original cooking time), can be plucked out of your fridge and zapped in your microwave. In 3 minutes you have a great tasting, low cost, low fat pasta dish—the answer to a tired person's prayer!

Makes 6 (5-ounce) servings

Appearance Result

Happy (because it's so easy to make!) and colorful.

Nutritional Analysis

Per (1-cup) Serving

WITH GROUND TURKEY: 228 Calories; 5 g Fat; 1 g Sat. Fat; 21 mg. Cholesterol; 244 mg Sodium; 32 g Carbohydrates; 1 g Fiber; 2 g Sugar; 13 g Protein.

WITH GROUND CHICKEN: 273 Calories; 6 g Fat; 2 g Sat. Fat; 53 mg Cholesterol; 271 mg Sodium; 32 g Carbohydrates; 1 g Fiber; 2 g Sugar; 21 g Protein.

Dee's Suggestions

This dish has storage power—about one and a half weeks in your refrigerator. It can also be frozen if desired. Before heating, I sometimes sprinkle a little grated parmesan or light mozzarella over the top. SO EASY—SO GOOD!

LOW FAT PASTA SENSATION

1½ pounds ground turkey (or 1½ pound ground chicken—white meat only)
2 large cooking onions
Paprika (to brown turkey or chicken)
4 cloves crushed garlic
1 tablespoon dried sweet basil
1 tablespoon oregano
3 tablespoons dried parsley flakes (for color)
½ teaspoon grated Parmesan cheese
Salt and pepper to taste
1 pound pasta (I use penne and shells, but choose any pasta you like, or combine several types for a better look)
1 (15-ounce) can and 1 (8-ounce) can tomato sauce

In a large nonstick pan, sauté turkey or chicken and onions until brown. Use paprika to add color and help brown. Add garlic, sweet basil, oregano, parsley and cheese. Salt and pepper to taste.

While mixture is browning, bring 4 quarts water to boil. Add pasta. Cook 10 to 12 minutes or until al dente (chewy, not soggy). Rinse in cold water and drain in colander.

Add tomato sauce to turkey or chicken mixture. Put pasta in a large bowl and add the meat mixture to the pasta.

PASTA SENSATION ZUCCHINI VARIATION

Another alternative pasta dish—again, only 20 minutes original cooking time. Because of the zucchini, this one has a lighter flavor than my original Pasta Sensation—great in the summer! And, in just 3 minutes from fridge to table, you have another yummy, no-fuss, low-fat pasta dish!

Makes 6 (8-ounce) servings.

Appearance Result

Sunny, colorful, orange-red sauce studded with zucchini slices and browned meat.

Nutritional Analysis

Per (8-ounce) serving: 482 Calories; 13 g Fat; 2 g Sat. Fat; 135 mg Cholesterol; 882 mg Sodium; 59 g Carbohydrates; 4 g Fiber; 7 g Sugar; 36 g Protein

Dee's Suggestions

Follow my original Pasta Sensation suggestions, and you can't lose. This dish can be stored for about one and a half weeks in your refrigerator and can also be frozen for longer storage.

PASTA SENSATION ZUCCHINI VARIATION

1 pound ground turkey or 1 pound ground chicken
2 large onions, chopped
2 medium zucchini, halved and sliced
4 cloves garlic, crushed
1 tablespoon dried sweet basil
1 tablespoon oregano
1 (16½-ounce) can stewed tomatoes
1 cup tomato sauce
Salt and pepper to taste
¼ cup Parmesan
½ cup shredded low-fat mozzarella
8 ounces uncooked pasta (penne, shells or rotini—plain or mixed)

In a large, nonstick pan, sauté turkey or chicken and onions until brown. Add zucchini, garlic, sweet basil and oregano. Add stewed tomatoes and sauce. Salt and pepper to taste.

While mixture is browning, bring 4 quarts water to boil. Add pasta. Cook 10 to 12 minutes or until al dente. Rinse in cold water and drain in colander.

When pasta is cooked, drain and add to the ground meat mixture. Before serving, add Parmesan and mozzarella and allow to melt into recipe.

Poultry, Meat, & Seafood

DEE'S NO-FRIED BREADED CHICKEN BREASTS

This is my very favorite recipe—for taste, appearance, versatility and speed. I give it a "10"! It is the best! It only takes 11 minutes to prepare 20 half breasts for your freezer using my method (I usually double this recipe and make 40 half breasts). This recipe retains its freshness and taste for up to three months in your freezer. Once frozen, the breasts can be quickly cooked in a toaster oven, conventional oven or microwave, tasting like you just made them. And there are so many ways to serve them. Once you make these, you'll love them as much as I do.

Makes 20 half breasts.

Appearance Result

Golden brown in color.

Nutritional Analysis

Per Serving (1 breast half): 326 Calories; 10.2 g Fat; 4.5 g Sat. Fat; 87 mg Cholesterol; 655 mg Sodium; 25 g Carbohydrates; 0 g Fiber; 2 g Sugar; 32 g Protein.

Dee's Suggestions

These breasts will serve up a variety of meals: •Great as an entrée with a side of pasta and a salad. •Slice into lengthwise strips and serve on top of your favorite salad greens. •As an entrée selection, these breasts go Italian. Cover with your favorite marinara sauce and sprinkle a little light mozzarella on top. •Maybe your mood is barbecue—spread your favorite low-fat barbecue sauce on top. •Pop onto a whole wheat bun with your favorite sandwich fixings, and make an incredibly delicious sandwich. •Last but not least, cut into chunks and serve with sweet and sour sauce—a wonderful appetizer for dinner guests. You will find, as I have, this recipe will make you a wizard, indeed!

Poultry, Meat, & Seafood

DEE'S NO-FRIED BREADED CHICKEN BREASTS

- 20 skinless, boneless half chicken breasts, slightly pounded
- 1 cup light Italian dressing (I prefer Paul Newman's)
- 1 stick butter, melted*
- ¼ stick light butter, melted*
- ¼ cup buttermilk
- 6 egg whites, beaten
- 3 cloves garlic, crushed
- 1 (21-ounce) box corn flake crumbs
- 5 tablespoons dried sweet basil
- 4 tablespoons dried oregano
- 2 tablespoons celery salt
- 2 tablespoons paprika
- 4 tablespoons dried parsley**

**Use fresh parsley if available. Wash, dry with paper towel, and chop.

Rinse chicken breasts and drain thoroughly in colander. In a large bowl, mix light Italian dressing, melted butter, buttermilk, beaten egg whites and garlic. In another large bowl, mix all dried ingredients except parsley.

Line a cookie sheet with foil. Dip chicken breasts in melted butter mixture and then dip into dried mixture. Coat breasts thoroughly. Lay approximately 10 breasts onto cookie sheet and sprinkle with parsley liberally. Separate layers with foil. Repeat laying breasts onto foil and sprinkle with parsley. Cookie sheet should be two layers high for 20 breasts—about 10 each layer.

Flash freeze breasts by placing entire cookie sheet with breasts UNCOVERED in your freezer. If your freezer is too narrow, split the number of breasts per foil layer and stack higher. Next day, remove chicken breasts from freezer. They'll be frozen solid and ready to be put unwrapped (no foil) in labeled, dated freezer bags. Return to freezer for up to 3 months.

When ready to cook, microwave on high for approximately 4 minutes, or bake in toaster oven 12 to 20 minutes at 450 degrees, or bake in conventional oven 20 to 25 minutes at 350 degrees.

GRILLED CHICKEN BREASTS

This tasty chicken breast recipe can be grilled or broiled in your oven. It's quick, versatile and low in fat. Because it freezes beautifully, you'll rely on it for many different kinds of meals. Certainly a help-mate to the tired and overworked—enjoy!

Makes 10 half chicken breasts.

Appearance Result
Slightly crusty outside, juicy inside.

Freezer Instructions
Let cool and then wrap each half chicken breast individually in foil. Place in labeled, dated zippered freezer bags, and freeze.

Nutritional Analysis
Per (4-ounce-breast) Serving: 154 Calories; 4 g Fat; 1 g Sat. Fat; 74 mg Cholesterol; 401 mg Sodium; 2 g Carbohydrates; 0 g Fiber; 0 g Sugars; 27 g Protein.

Dee's Suggestions
I use my chicken breasts as an entrée, accompanied by pasta or potato salad, etc. You can also eat them cold, or micro-wave after defrosted to reheat. They're also great on a toasted whole wheat bun, layered with romaine lettuce, a slice of onion, and some honey-mustard sauce. YUM!

GRILLED CHICKEN BREASTS

10 half breasts—skinless, boneless, lightly pounded (I get them from my butcher this way, but you can pound them yourself)
1 cup low-cal Italian dressing (your favorite brand)
1 tablespoon dried sweet basil

Mix the Italian dressing and basil in a bowl. Add the chicken breasts. Marinate overnight, mixing occasionally, if possible.

If grilling, spray grill with cooking spray before using so breasts don't stick. Grilling should only take about six minutes on each side. I advise you to watch as you grill—every grill is different, which may change the cooking time. It's important that you don't overcook, or the breasts will be too dry. If broiling in the oven, use a broiling pan, and cook approximately six minutes on each side.

LEMON CHICKEN

Chicken, how do I love thee? Let me count the ways! This chicken variation is love at first bite. This tangy, 10-minute miracle looks almost as good as it tastes!

Makes 6 servings.

Appearance Result
Golden brown outside, tender-white inside.

Nutritional Analysis
Per (4-ounce) serving: 253.5 Calories; 7.0 g Fat; 0.2 g Sat. Fat; 73 g Cholesterol; 595 mg Sodium; 15.9 g Carbohydrates; 0 g Fiber; 2.5 g Sugar; 30.9 g Protein

Dee's Suggestions
I serve this hot as an entrée with a vegetable and salad. Any leftovers make a nice chicken sandwich.

LEMON CHICKEN

6 boneless, skinless half chicken breasts, lightly pounded
½ cup Egg Beaters
⅔ cup lemon juice
1 teaspoon salt
½ teaspoon black pepper
1 tablespoon plus 1 teaspoon olive oil
2 tablespoons dry sweet basil
1 cup bread crumbs

Mix Egg Beaters, lemon juice, salt and pepper in a bowl. Add chicken and marinate for 15 minutes (or longer—overnight even—the longer it marinates, the more flavorful the chicken). Heat oil in nonstick skillet. Mix sweet basil and bread crumbs together and dredge chicken in mixture. Sauté 5 minutes each side or until done.

EFFORTLESS ROASTED HERBED CHICKEN

When I say effortless, this chicken is it! And it tastes fabulous. Depending on the size of your family, you may want to cook two chickens at the same time. This will yield a variety of prepared meals for at least a full week. How wonderful to come home at the end of a long, busy day to a delicious chicken dinner—ready for your table in just minutes!

Appearance Result

Crusty brown on the outside, juicy and tender on the inside.

Nutritional Analysis

Per (4-ounce) Serving (with skin removed): 120 Calories; 5 g Fat; 1 g Sat. Fat, 50 g Cholesterol; 46 mg Sodium; 1 g Carbohydrates 0 g Fiber; 0 g Sugar; 18 g Protein.

Dee's Suggestions

This recipe is very versatile. It can be served as is, carved hot from the oven, as a main dish. It's also marvelous covered with your favorite barbecue sauce and heated. Serving it cold is another option, or slice the chicken for a sandwich or add to a salad served with great bread. Go for it! You'll love it!

EFFORTLESS ROASTED HERBED CHICKEN

4 to 5 pound roasting chicken, whole
2 tablespoons olive oil
1 tablespoon sweet basil
1 tablespoon oregano
1 tablespoon rosemary
1 tablespoon paprika
1 teaspoon celery salt*
½ teaspoon tarragon
½ teaspoon thyme
¼ teaspoon sage
1 tablespoon parsley flakes or 1 package fresh parsley, if available
¼ teaspoon coarsely ground pepper

*Optional.

Preheat oven to 400 degrees. Soak the bird in a large bowl of water for about 10 minutes, making sure the inside cavity is well cleaned. Rinse, pat dry. In a small bowl, mix the olive oil and dry ingredients. This mixture will be a paste-like consistency. Cover all sides of the chicken well with the mixture. If you're using the fresh parsley, wash, drain, pat dry, coarsely chop and sprinkle over chicken. This gives the recipe added color and taste—a quick gourmet look. This chicken recipe is best cooked in the oven on a vertical chicken roasting stand, allowing most of the fat to drain away from the chicken; if not available, use a regular roasting rack and pan. Cook uncovered in a preheated 400 degree oven for 20 minutes; cover with foil, and lower heat to 350 degrees for about 1½ hours, depending on your oven. Remove the skin after cooking to reduce the fat.

MOLONARI'S CHICKEN WITH PORTOBELLO MUSHROOMS

Feel like showing off your cooking talents? Then this chicken entrée is for you. I promise, after you serve this dish, people will treat you differently.

Makes 4 servings.

Nutritional Analysis

Per (4-ounce breast) Serving: 349 Calories; 8 g Fat; 2 g Sat. Fat, 96 g Cholesterol; 224 mg Sodium; 26 g Carbohydrates; 13 g Fiber; 1 g Sugar; 41 g Protein.

Dee's Suggestions

This delicious recipe is a great main dish to a most elegant meal. I would serve it with my favorite salad and steaming bread.

MOLONARI'S CHICKEN WITH PORTOBELLO MUSHROOMS

1 tablespoon olive oil

Salt and pepper to taste

4 (4-ounce) skinless chicken breasts, pounded thin

4 tablespoons flour

1 pound fresh cleaned spinach

1 pound portobello mushrooms, sliced

Juice from 2 lemons

1 tablespoon fresh minced garlic

4 ounces dry white wine

Heat the olive oil in a nonstick pan. Dredge the salted and peppered chicken breasts in flour and shake off the excess. Place in the skillet and cook 3 minutes. Turn the breasts and cook 3 minutes more. While the chicken is cooking, wash the spinach leaves in a salad spinner, spinning off all the excess water. Add the sliced portobellos, lemon juice, spinach, garlic, and white wine to the skillet and cook, covered, 1 minute to wilt spinach. Remove the chicken to warm plates. Continue cooking the mushroom and spinach mixture until the liquid in the skillet is reduced and thicker. Spoon over the chicken breasts and serve.

CHICKEN "SLOPPY DEE'S"

Move over sloppy joes, Chicken "Sloppy Dee's" is stealing your thunder. This update on a mainstream American Classic is lower in fat, easier to make, and just as tasty as its predecessor. This is the perfect meal remedy for a tired soul.

Makes 1 serving.

Appearance Result

Golden brown studded with red and green

Nutritional Analysis

Per Serving: 360 Calories; 12 g Fat; 2.7 g Sat. Fat; 83 g Cholesterol; 100 mg Sodium; 15.8 g Carbohydrates; 2.9 g Fiber; 1.0 g Sugar; 40.9 g Protein

Dee's Suggestions

Spoon over a toasted wheat bun. Top with drizzled ketchup to add tomato flavor.

CHICKEN "SLOPPY DEE'S"

Pam olive oil
1 teaspoon olive oil
½ cup onion (sliced, diced—anyway you like it)
½ cup diced red sweet pepper
½ cup diced green pepper
1 fresh garlic cloves, crushed*
Salt and pepper to taste
6 ounces ground chicken breast—white meat only

*Add more garlic if desired.

Spray nonstick skillet with Pam olive oil. Heat olive oil in skillet. Sauté onions, peppers and garlic until onions are translucent (about 10 minutes), spraying with additional Pam olive oil as needed. Add seasoned chicken and sauté until done—approximately 8 minutes, again spraying with additional Pam as needed.

ROASTED TURKEY BREAST

Lot's of healthy protein and low in fat, this versatile roast has staying power—a week's worth of lunches and dinners. And, oh, so easy!!

Makes 10 servings.

Appearance Result
Crusty brown outside, juicy white meat inside.

Nutritional Analysis
Per (4-ounce) serving: 180 Calories; 6.5 g Fat; 2.2 g Sat. Fat; 62 g Cholesterol; 72 mg Sodium; 1.7 g Carbohydrates; 0 g Fiber; 0 g Sugar; 29.3 Protein

Dee's Suggestions
This tasty dish makes a wonderful entrée. Slice it cold for a sandwich; cut it in strips, wrap in foil and take to work for a fat-burning protein snack; chunk it, add light mayonnaise for a low-fat turkey salad; use strips over greens for a main-dish salad; I could go on and on and on.... ★

ROASTED TURKEY BREAST

1 (3-pound) turkey breast
1 tablespoon olive oil
2 tablespoons **Dee's Magic Mix** (you may use more if desired)

Preheat oven to 400 degrees for 20 minutes then reduce to 325. Wash turkey breast and dry thoroughly with paper towels. Rub dry breast with oil and sprinkle with Dee's Magic Mix. Cook 30 minutes per pound. Remove skin before eating.

GRILLED TURKEY—GOBBLE, GOBBLE—ALL YEAR 'ROUND

This may sound strange to you turkey traditionalists, but once you eat turkey that's been prepared on the grill, you'll never want to eat it any other way. When compared to conventional oven roasting, the bird cooks in half the time. What's more, the meat has a juicy grilled flavor that you just can't get from oven-roasting. This is an easy, low-fat recipe that I serve five or six times a year. My grilled turkey is definitely not just for Thanksgiving!

Appearance Result

Crusty golden brown outside, really juicy—not dry, inside.

Nutritional Analysis

Per (4-ounce) Serving: 333 Calories; 11 g Fat; 3.3 g Sat. Fat; 139 mg Cholesterol; 129 mg Sodium; 1.7 g Carbohydrates; 0 g Fiber; 0 g Sugars; 53.5 g Protein.

Dee's Suggestions

I usually buy a 12- to 13- pound turkey, which yields lots of great, low-fat meals for Craig and me. After about a week of turkey sandwiches and turkey sliced over greens, I carve what's leftover and freeze for more good food fast.

GRILLED TURKEY—GOBBLE, GOBBLE—ALL YEAR 'ROUND

1 (12-pound) fresh turkey
4 tablespoons olive oil
4 tablespoons dried oregano
4 tablespoons dried sweet basil
4 tablespoons paprika
1 tablespoon celery salt
1 tablespoon thyme
2 tablespoons garlic powder
Large disposable aluminum roasting pan

Preheat gas grill on high. If using charcoal grill, let coals get very hot.

Wash the bird thoroughly and pat dry. Brush olive oil over the outside of the turkey with a pastry brush.

Mix all dry ingredients in a bowl, then sprinkle over the olive-oil-coated bird. Place the bird in the aluminum roasting pan. Add 2 cups water to the bottom of the pan; replenish water as it evaporates during cooking.

Place the pan on preheated grill and lower the grill top. Grill 20 minutes on high, sealing in the seasonings. Then reduce the grill heat to medium/low, depending on grill size and performance. Keep adding more water to the bottom of the pan as needed, so the bird won't get dry. Cooking time will be about 15 minutes per pound weight.

Note: Since every grill is different, use your judgment on heat level and cooking time. If your grill cooks very hot, cook bird on low instead of medium.

When bird is done, remove pan from the grill and place bird on carving board. Let stand about 10 minutes before carving. Be sure to remove the skin before eating.

SUNDAY TURKEY MEAT LOAF

I can't believe it's Sunday! What should I make for Sunday family dinner? Look no further. This meatloaf is sure to please your brood. Flavorful and satisfying. If you're lucky, you'll have some left over for Monday.

Makes 4 servings.

Appearance Result

A golden brown meatloaf.

Nutritional Analysis

Per (4-ounce) serving: 305 Calories; 11.9 g Fat; 3.25 g Sat. Fat; 90 g Cholesterol; 514 mg Sodium; 20.8 g Carbohydrates; 1.5 g Fiber; 3.75 g Sugar; 29.8 g Protein

Dee's Suggestions

Slice and serve warm for dinner; cold for sandwiches the next day.

SUNDAY TURKEY MEAT LOAF

1 pound ground turkey breast
1 small onion, diced
1 sweet red pepper, diced (optional)
½ cup wheat bread crumbs
½ cup Ragu Sauce (or any pasta sauce)
1 (4-ounce) carton Egg Beaters (= 2 eggs)
2 tablespoons dried parsley (or ½ cup fresh Italian parsley, chopped)
1 tablespoon light soy sauce
½ teaspoon ground pepper
1 teaspoon dry sweet basil
2 cloves garlic, crushed

Preheat oven to 350 degrees. Spray a 10 x 6½-inch baking pan with Pam and set aside. Place all ingredients in a large bowl and use your hands to mix gently until well combined. Shape the turkey mixture into a loaf and place in pan. Bake until firm to the touch, about 40 minutes.

ROASTED LEG OF LAMB—FOR LAMB-LOVERS ONLY

This is a great "show-off" dish—wonderful for a holiday or very special dinner. Don't forget to make sure the lamb is well trimmed of all fat. And remember, because it's a meat dish, watch your portion. When company comes for dinner, this dish is sure to label you "Gourmet Cook"!

Makes 12 servings.

Appearance Result

Crusty coating on the outside, tender and juicy inside.

Nutritional Analysis

Per (5-ounce) Serving: 298 Calories; 12.4 g Fat; 4.6 g Sat. Fat; 134 mg Cholesterol; 100 mg Sodium; 4.9 g Carbohydrates; 0.1 g Fiber; 0.7 g Sugar; 40.4 g Protein.

Dee's Suggestions

This wonderful entrée goes beautifully with my garlic mashed potatoes. Leftovers can be frozen for other great meals.

ROASTED LEG OF LAMB—FOR LAMB-LOVERS ONLY

1 (6 to 8-pound) leg of spring lamb, bone-in, sirloin cut off, trimmed of all visible fat, but with outer membrane intact
1¼ cups lemon juice
4 cloves crushed garlic
6 tablespoons fresh ginger, grated
1 teaspoon dried thyme
Freshly ground black pepper
2 teaspoons olive oil

In a large, heavyweight zippered bag, combine the lemon juice, garlic and ginger. Place the meat inside the bag with the marinade mixture. Refrigerate overnight or for at least three hours.

Preheat oven to 450 degrees.

Mix thyme and several grindings of black pepper together in a small bowl. Remove lamb from marinade bag. Brush lamb with olive oil and rub the seasoning mixture over the entire leg. Place the lamb on a rack in a roasting pan. Insert a meat thermometer in the fleshiest part of the leg.

Cook 30 minutes in a preheated 450 degree oven, then turn down the oven to 350 and cook until the meat thermometer reaches your desired doneness—rare, medium or well done. It's not necessary to baste.

When lamb has reached your desired doneness, remove form oven and let leg rest on a cutting board for 15 to 20 minutes before carving.

QUICK OPEN FACE MAIN MEAL SANDWICH

A dish that fulfills the very underrated emotional satisfaction of chewing. Here's a beautiful dish that even looks great on a paper plate. You'll make big points with this one!

Makes three servings.

Appearance Result

Very colorful—a great meal presentation!

Nutritional Analysis

Per Serving (9½-ounce sandwich): 401 Calories; 11 g Fat; 3 g. Sat. Fat; 165 mg Cholesterol; 529 mg Sodium; 40.2 g Carbohydrates; 1.8 g Fiber; 5.7 g Sugar; 33.7 g Protein.

Dee's Suggestions

This is a very filling sandwich; it's more than a sandwich—it's a full meal! You have protein, veggies and carbohydrates in one dish. Because it's so quick and easy, I think you'll learn to count on it year-round. It's especially nice in hot weather, because you don't use your oven.

OVEN MEAL No. 3

Yield; — 6 SERVINGS

MEAT LOAF

BAKED POTATOES   STEAMED SQUASH

NUT BREAD
STUFFED BAKED APPLES

Time: 1 ½ hours   Temperature: 350° F.

MEAT LOAF

OVEN MEAL No. 4

Yield; — 6 SERVINGS

ROAST DUCK
ORANGE SWEET POTATO STUFFING
CARROTS AND CELERY   CREAMED ONIONS AU GRATIN
LATTICE APPLE PIE

Time: 1 ¾ hours   Temperature: 350° F.

ROAST DUCK
with Orange Sweet Potato Stuffing

QUICK OPEN FACE MAIN MEAL SANDWICH

- 1 green bell pepper
- 1 red bell pepper
- 1 large red onion
- 1 pound ground turkey*
- 2 cloves garlic, crushed
- 2 teaspoons oregano
- Paprika for color
- Salt and pepper to taste
- Ciabatta bread
- 1 tablespoon light mozzarella cheese

Slice green and red peppers and onions in rings. In medium-size nonstick skillet, sauté peppers, onion and the ground turkey. Add fresh crushed garlic and oregano. Sprinkle paprika while browning. Add salt and pepper to taste. Sauté until vegetables are soft and turkey is golden brown in color.

While mixture is cooking, cut ciabatta bread lengthwise, then cut into 4-inch lengths and toast.

When mixture is cooked, spoon onto toasted bread. Sprinkle ° teaspoon cheese over each piece. Put sandwich in toaster oven or microwave to melt the cheese.

*I prefer dark meat ground turkey because it's very moist. But using white meat ground turkey, as I've done here, will yield a recipe that's lower in fat. The choice is yours.

LEAN MARINATED ROAST PORK LOIN

This entrée is an excellent, low fat choice—great for Sunday dinner. You may not think "pork" when you think "low fat," but the boneless center cut of the loin is as lean as they come. Because it's so flavorful, you only need a moderate portion. I promise you rave reviews.

Makes 8 (4-ounce) servings.

Appearance Result

Slices are light tan inside covered with a burgundy glaze.

Nutritional Analysis

Per Serving (4 ounces) : 298 Calories; 10 g Fat; 3 g Sat. Fat; 87 mg Cholesterol; 771 mg Sodium; 19 g Carbohydrates; 32 g Protein.

Dee's Suggestions

I usually serve this dish with my spinach mashed potatoes, and my cranberry relish or applesauce. This dish is very versatile. You can freeze leftovers for another meal or opt to store in the fridge. It can then be made very quickly into a hearty pork sandwich served on a nutritious multi-grain bun. Once it's made, you're just minutes away from another great meal.

LEAN MARINATED ROAST PORK LOIN

3 pounds boneless loin pork roast, center cut, well trimmed so all visible fat is removed
⅓ cup dried mustard*
¼ cup dried thyme*
½ cup medium sherry
½ cup low sodium soy sauce
3 fresh garlic cloves, finely chopped
3 tablespoons grated fresh ginger
6 ounces currant jelly
1 tablespoon soy sauce

*Use enough to cover outside of roast—you may need more or less.

Preheat oven to 325 degrees. Wash the pork loin and pat dry. Rub meat with dry mustard and thyme on all sides. In small bowl, combine sherry, soy sauce, garlic and ginger. Place meat in a large plastic bag, pour in the marinade, fasten securely and refrigerate 2 to 3 hours, turning the bag several times.

Remove the meat from the bag and cook on a roasting rack in a roasting pan. Allow 25 minutes per pound or until internal temperature of 145 degrees is reached—take with a meat thermometer. Baste occasionally with the marinade. When done, remove meat to a board to cool.

For glaze, melt the currant jelly in a small saucepan over medium heat. When bubbly, add 1 tablespoon soy sauce. Let glaze cook until smooth, stirring constantly. Spoon over the pork roast and continue to let cool to room temperature. Slice and serve, pouring leftover glaze over the slices.

LEAN RUMP ROAST

A no-time cooking experience to satisfy your meat cravings. From this basic recipe, you can produce many meals—all in 20 minutes preparation time (or less)!

Appearance Result

A slight crusty coating on the outer layer, tender and juicy inside.

Nutritional Analysis

Per (4-ounce) Serving: 140 Calories; 4 g Fat; 1 g Sat. Fat; 40 mg Cholesterol; 105 mg sodium; 1 g Carbohydrates; 0 g Fiber; 0 g Sugars; 18 g Protein.

Dee's Suggestions

I recommend this dish "as-is" for a wonderful main event. Depending on how many people you serve, you may have a sufficient quantity left over, which can be frozen to be used as an entrée later. Another option is to take the remaining roast meat and slice for delicious sandwiches, or sliced over a main-dish salad for other meals during the week.

LEAN RUMP ROAST

2½ pounds rump roast
2 cups red wine (any dry red wine will do)
3 cloves crushed garlic
1 tablespoon low sodium soy sauce
1 tablespoon olive oil
1 teaspoon sweet basil
1 teaspoon paprika
1 teaspoon oregano
1 teaspoon tarragon
1 teaspoon garlic powder
1 teaspoon celery salt
1 teaspoon dried parsley flakes
¼ teaspoon ground pepper
5 scallions, chopped

Wash the meat and pat dry with a paper towel. Place meat in a large plastic freezer bag; add the wine and crushed garlic. Close the bag and store overnight in the refrigerator. Marinating the meat in this way makes it tender and flavorful.

Preheat oven to 400 degrees. Mix soy sauce, olive oil, dry ingredients and scallions in a small bowl. The mixture will be almost the consistency of paste. Remove the rump roast from the plastic bag. With a pastry brush, apply mixture on all sides of the meat. Place on a baking rack in a shallow baking pan. Cook uncovered in a preheated 400 degree oven for 20 minutes. Then reduce the heat to 300 degrees, cover the roast with foil and cook until done. Use a meat thermometer to cook the roast to your desired taste—rare, medium or well done.

TUNA CAKES

This recipe creates a whole new way to serve canned tuna. Once you make this quantity, you're home free for lots of tasty meals from freezer to table.

Makes 20 (5-ounce) patties.

Appearance Result
Colorful and crispy golden brown.

Nutritional Analysis
Per Serving (5-ounce patty): 255 Calories; 6 g Fat; 1 g Sat. Fat; 45 mg Cholesterol; 118 mg Sodium; 17 g Carbohydrates; 2 g Fiber; 2 g Sugar; 32 g Protein.

Dee's Suggestions
I love serving this recipe with my garlic mashed potatoes—a great combination! It takes about an hour to make up all 20 tuna cakes, but think of all the 20-minute meals you'll have at your fingertips. Thaw tuna cakes in your refrigerator or microwave, but keep chilled in the fridge at least 15 minutes before cooking. Enjoy!

TUNA CAKES

6 cans (large, 12.25-ounce cans) solid white tuna in water
1½ cups (16-ounce jar) sweet pickle relish
3 cups chopped green onions
3 cups red bell pepper, chopped
1¼ teaspoons black pepper
1 tablespoon dried sweet basil
6 beaten egg whites
2¾ cups cornflake crumbs, divided
2 cups Dijon mustard
½ cup + 2 tablespoons Hellmann's Reduced Fat Mayonnaise
Paprika

Open tuna cans, rinse in colander, drain thoroughly and put into large bowl. Empty pickle relish into strainer—drain thoroughly. Add to tuna. Break up mixture with large spoon. Chop onions and red bell peppers and add to mixture. Add black pepper and sweet basil. Beat egg whites; add to mixture. Add 2 cups of cornflake crumbs, mustard, and mayonnaise to mix. Thoroughly mix all ingredients together with large spoon.

Shape into 2-inch balls. On a cutting board, spread remaining cornflake crumbs. Roll balls in cornflake crumbs, covering well (add more cornflake crumbs to cover all balls, if needed). Flatten into midsize patties. Refrigerate 30 minutes.

When ready to cook, sauté tuna cakes in a nonstick skillet sprayed with olive oil cooking spray on medium heat (or use a small amount of olive oil—1 teaspoon*). Cook 5 minutes on each side, or until golden brown, sprinkling paprika on the patties for color. Remove from skillet, and drain on paper towels. Wrap remainder of patties individually in foil. Place in labeled zippered freezer bags and freeze.

*If olive oil is used, the fat grams per serving increase slightly.

Desserts

YOGURT APPLESAUCE PARFAIT

A dressed-up dessert with down-home country apple taste. This cool, creamy treat is a special ending to any meal. And best of all, it's NO FAT!

Makes 1 serving.

Appearance Result

Layered in a parfait glass—like a trifle.

Nutritional Analysis

Per Serving: 76.5 Calories; 0 g Fat; 0 g Sat. Fat; 0 g Cholesterol; 15 mg Sodium; 18.6 g Carbohydrates; 0 g Fiber; 18.6 g Sugar; 7 g Protein

Dee's Suggestions

Go For It!!!!!

YOGURT APPLESAUCE PARFAIT

2 tablespoons chunky applesauce
½ teaspoon honey, drizzled
1 tablespoon non-fat French vanilla yogurt
½ teaspoon honey, drizzled
4 tablespoons chunky applesauce
Nutmeg

Layer ingredients in order listed. Sprinkle with nutmeg.

APPLE SQUARES

The best movie in town is playing right in your own kitchen. Fresh apple squares only take minutes to mix up and will stay fresh and moist for at least a week. It also plays a double feature, for it can be eaten as a breakfast cake. Definitely a happy ending!

Makes 24 (2-inch) squares.

Appearance Result

Toasty brown, studded with lots of apples that have risen to the top.

Nutritional Analysis

Per Serving (one square): 119 Calories; 0.4 g Fat; 0.1 g Sat. Fat; 0 g Cholesterol; 45 mg Sodium; 28.3 g Carbohydrates; 1.5 g Fiber, 2 g Protein

Dee's Suggestions

This recipe is truly amazing. Because of the apples, it never loses moisture. A week later, it tastes like you just made it—an Oscar performance!

APPLE SQUARES

2 cups flour
1 teaspoon baking soda
1 teaspoon cinnamon
1 (4-ounce) carton Egg Beaters (2 eggs)
1¼ cups sugar
1 cup orange juice
4 to 6 Granny Smith apples, peeled and sliced medium thickness
½ cup nuts (optional)
½ cup raisins (optional)

Combine all ingredients and mix well. Spray a 9x13-inch pan with nonstick cooking spray and spread ingredients in pan. Bake at 350 degrees for 1 hour. Let cool and store covered at room temperature.

"PUDDING ON THE RITZ" LEMON MOUSSE

This dish is an easy but elegant French mousse dessert. Don't let the "mousse" intimidate you—it only takes minutes to prepare. This creamy smooth, lemony delight will make you feel like company, and it's perfect to serve to company!

Makes 12 (½-cup) servings

Appearance Result

Pale lemon yellow, smooth and creamy.

Nutritional Analysis

Per Serving (½ cup): 167 Calories; 2.3 g Fat; 2.3 g Sat. Fat; 0 g Cholesterol; 97 mg Sodium; 33.4 g Carbohydrates; 0 g Fiber; 24.5 g Sugars; 1.7 g Protein

Dee's Suggestions

Serve this yummy dessert in any type of goblet. Garnish with grated lemon peel or a sprig of mint. Keep portion in mind when serving this dessert—a half-cup serving is very satisfying.

"PUDDING ON THE RITZ" LEMON MOUSSE

2 (2.9-ounce) boxes Lemon Jell-O Cook & Serve Pudding & Pie Filling
1 cup sugar
½ cup lemon juice
1 (8-ounce) carton Egg Beaters (4 eggs)
4 cups water
1 (8-ounce) carton Lite Cool Whip topping

Stir pudding mix, sugar, lemon juice and Egg Beaters in medium saucepan. Stir in water. Cook on medium heat, stirring constantly, until mixture comes to a full boil. Remove from heat and cool 30 minutes (for faster cooling, put in refrigerator). Once cooled, fold in Cool Whip. Serve in individual ½-cup servings and top with grated lemon peel.

MORE DESSERT SUGGESTIONS FROM DEE

I haven't ventured very far into the wide world of baking and creating fabulous desserts, because most are naturally high in fat and calories. Following, however, are some simple, low-fat foods that are quick and easy to serve that satisfy my sweet tooth.

Most of the following dessert suggestions are very low in fat. When I build a dessert, I allow 4 fat grams maximum per serving. Remember to read labels and choose low-fat items—and always remember moderation! A single portion of any one of these items is very satisfying.

Here are some of my suggestions:

ANGEL FOOD CAKE

Angel food cake has virtually no fat. I use it in so many different ways. In seconds, you can serve a treat that looks beautiful and tastes great. Angel food cake can be found fresh-baked in many supermarkets. I buy extra and freeze it for convenience—when I'm in the mood for cake.

Remember, presentation means so much. Serving this cake on a glass plate really improves the look—and, somehow, the taste as well.

SUGGESTIONS:
- Serve a slice with your favorite berries on top—and a dollop of lite or fat-free whipped topping.
- Try a slice with a scoop of nonfat frozen yogurt.
- Serve a slice with fat-free pudding on top—chocolate is really yummy!

FRUIT CUPS

Makeup a delicious fruit cup from your favorite fruit selections. Try berries, cantaloupe, watermelon, honeydew melon, fresh pineapple, grapes, bananas, etc. Again, most fruits have almost no fat.

Slice and/or cube these fruits and serve them in a parfait glass or wine goblet with a fat-free whipped topping. Garnish with mint leaves. What a great look and taste!

JELLO FAT-FREE PUDDING SNACK

In my opinion, this is the only fat-free pudding that has taste—and I've tried them all! One serving has 100 calories and ZERO fat grams and cholesterol—and it really does taste good! I like chocolate, but sometimes I get in the mood for vanilla. Serve them in glass goblets for that special touch. I like to swirl chocolate and vanilla together—looks fantastic and tastes great!

I CAN'T BELIEVE IT'S YOGURT

Again, this is my favorite yogurt-chain yogurt—great for that Saturday night after-dinner treat. They have many nonfat choices that are just delicious! What's more, they also have hot fudge and caramel topping—FAT FREE! And they taste so yummy with no aftertaste. Try them all—you'll love them!

SORBETS

Fruit sorbets are a great, low-fat selection. I chill wine goblets in the freezer, to give them a frosty glaze. When I'm ready for a special, low-fat dessert, I take them out and put in a scoop of sorbet and garnish with mint leaves, berries, or grapes. Impressive—and so cool and tasty.

Chapter Five

EXERCISE:
THE KEY TO WELLNESS

I know what you're thinking. "This is a cookbook! Why is she wasting my time on exercise?"

First of all, without exercise, I wouldn't be the person I am today. I wouldn't be enjoying my current good health and overall well-being. I wouldn't have the energy level I need to get me through the day. I couldn't possibly maintain my size and shape, or look and feel good in my clothes.

In my quest for personal wellness, I realized that regular exercise was critical to maintain my optimal health—physical, mental and spiritual. Exercise is the key to total wellness. Studies have shown that a regular exercise routine (3 times a week, 20 minutes each time) helps decrease the risk of cardiovascular disease, hypertension, obesity and high blood cholesterol. People with adequate fitness levels generally have more stamina and energy, less fatigue and fewer risks for certain types of injuries.

How can you begin a healthy, safe exercise routine? Think of me as your own personal trainer. I've developed an exercise strategy for three basic types of people:

1.) The Frenzied Person

2.) The Person with Minimal Time

3.) The Person Who Can Make the Time

Most of you will fit into one of these three categories. Many of you may be frenzied one week and have more time the next. Whatever your situation, YOU, TOO CAN FIT EXERCISE INTO YOUR OVERALL WELLNESS PROGRAM. If I can do it, so can you! It's not as grueling as you think, either.

Let's define these three categories. If you're a **Frenzied Person**, you have absolutely NO time on your hands. Whether you're in a fast-paced world at work, or racing around playing taxi driver for your kids and maintaining your home, everything else has become a priority in your life—everything but YOU!

The **Person with Minimal Time** is juggling lots of things at once, too, but is able to set aside three nonconsecutive half-hours during the week for yourself.

Finally, if you're a **Person Who Can Make the Time**, you are able to set aside three to six hours during the week for exercise.

One more thing before we get into my four steps to an effective workout. Once you begin to see the benefits of regular exercise, many "Frenzied People" I know have turned into "People Who Make the Time." Feeling good perpetuates itself.

FOUR STEPS TO AN EFFECTIVE WORKOUT
STEP I—HEALTH HISTORY QUESTIONNAIRE

The following short questionnaire identifies the small number of adults for whom physical activity may be inappropriate, or those who should seek medical advice concerning the type of activity most suitable to their condition. If you answer yes to any question, I advise that you postpone exercise until you've received your doctor's approval.

HEALTH HISTORY QUESTIONNAIRE

1. Has your doctor ever told you that you have heart trouble?
2. Do you frequently suffer from pains in your chest?
3. Do you often feel faint or have spells of severe dizziness?
4. Have you ever been diagnosed with high blood pressure?
5. Have you ever been diagnosed with bone or joint problems such as arthritis that have been aggravated by exercise or might be made worse by exercise?
6. Are there any other physical reasons not mentioned here which would impede you from following a program of regular exercise?
7. Are you over age 65 and not accustomed to exercising?

STEP II—THE FITNESS TRIANGLE

There are three sides to my fitness triangle. 1.) Cardiovascular Training; 2.) Weight Training; and 3.) Flexibility Training. All three are important components of a healthy exercise program.

1.) CARDIOVASCULAR TRAINING

Commonly know as aerobic fitness, cardiovascular training is the ability to persist or sustain an activity for an extended period of time while stressing the lungs, heart and circulatory system. Cardio exercises like walking and biking are great for your heart and lungs and help stimulate your metabolism and burn fat.

I've always said that the best aerobic exercise is the one you do consistently. Some of you may prefer to hit the great outdoors and walk, so the only equipment you'll need is a good pair of shoes. Swimming is another excellent way of aerobic training, requiring only consistent movement for 20 minutes in the water—and a bathing suit.

While I don't advocate any one type of equipment, here's a good basic list of equipment you may wish to try out:

Treadmills—motorized or not. Used for walking or jogging.

Stationary Bicycle—low impact. The seat should be high enough so that when your leg is at full extension, you still have a slight knee bend.

Cross-country Ski Machines—again, low impact

Rowing Machines—low impact, yet again. Be sure to find a model that doesn't stress the lower back excessively.

2. WEIGHT TRAINING

With the primary goal of strengthening and toning your muscles, weight resistance will also improve circulation, build strength and endurance, replace fat with muscle, and just make you feel better overall.

Before you begin any weight training program, get advice from an expert. Whether at a health club or gym or by hiring a professional trainer at home, it's important to get individualized help. A few sessions with an exercise specialist will give you maximum results in the shortest period of time. And you'll be less likely to injure yourself if you're trained to use weights properly.

If you can't get to a club or gym or hire a trainer, the next best thing is to rent or buy a weight training videotape. *Shape Magazine* often rates current videos which may help you select one from the wide variety on the market. Or try several by renting them and following along. Then select your personal favorite.

When you're ready to weight train, be sure to warm up and stretch first. A 5-to-10-minute cardio-vascular warm-up is ideal, helping the blood circulate and warming the muscles, easing muscle strain.

Be sure to take it easy and set your own pace. Don't try to keep up with anyone else. Pay special attention to previous injuries. If it hurts, don't work through the pain. Switch to exercises that aren't painful but work the same muscle groups. And don't worry about your body weight. Muscle is more dense and weighs more than fat, so you may be getting thinner, but not lighter.

Finally, weight training should be performed 2 to 3 times a week, ideally, being sure to rest a day in between weight training sessions. Muscles need rest in order to develop and tone properly.

3. FLEXIBILITY TRAINING

Stretching, or moving your limbs to a point where there is a slight discomfort in the muscle and supporting connective tissue, is the third essential component of a total exercise program. The object is to reduce muscle tension, thereby promoting freer movement. Stretching should not be stressful, but peaceful, relaxing and noncompetitive. The subtle, invigorating feeling of stretching allows you to get in touch with your muscles.

The key to stretching is regularity. Everyone, regardless of age or flexibility, should stretch. You don't need to be in top physical condition to enjoy its benefits. Stretching should be tailored to your particular muscular structure and flexibility. If you have serious physical problems or a recent surgery, check with your doctor before you begin a stretching regimen.

Stretching should be done every time you exercise, at the end of your warm-up or at the end of your exercise session. Hold each stretch for a minimum of 10 to 30 seconds. Never bounce while stretching.

The professional at your club or gym or your trainer can help you tailor a stretching regimen just for you. There are many books and videos available on stretching as well. Find one that you like and follow the suggested movements.

STEP III—DETERMINING YOUR TARGET TRAINING ZONE

Responses to aerobic exercise vary considerably from person to person, so workout intensity varies as well. You'll need to determine your cardiovascular exercise intensity to be sure you're training within your target zone, the healthiest and most optimal range for training.

The best way to determine your aerobic intensity is by finding your Target Heart Rate (THR). This measurement is the level at which you should perform all of your cardiovascular exercise—walking, biking, swimming, etc.

Your body needs oxygen to burn fat. Training should be done at around 60% of your maximum heart rate for optimal results. The closer you are to 60%, the more fat you'll burn. The THR range is anything between 60 and 85% of your Maximum Heart Rate. The best aerobic exercise is a sustained workout within this range for at least 20 minutes.

Anything above your Maximum Heart Rate will no longer be aerobic, because you're no longer using oxygen at this level. You shouldn't work out at a level where you're uncomfortable and unable to sustain for at least 20 minutes. Remember, never exceed 85% of your Maximum Heart Rate to stay aerobic and burn fat.

To determine your THR, follow this simple formula:

220 - your age = Maximum Heart Rate (MHR)

MHR X .6 = 60% of your MHR

MHR X .85 = 85% of your MHR

The formula above helps you determine your training zone. Let's use an example of a woman who's 41 years old:

220 - 41 = 179 MHR

179 X .6 = 107

179 X .85 = 152

By plugging in the formula, we know that this woman's training zone is between 107 and 152 heart beats per minute. When she takes her pulse during exercise, her beats per minute should fall within 107 and 152 to be aerobic and burn fat.

72 and 85

STEP IV—MEASURING YOUR HEART RATE

Your heart rate can be found by taking your pulse or by using a heart rate monitor (found at a sporting goods store). You can take your pulse in your neck (carotid artery) or your wrist (radial artery). The carotid pulse may be felt by gently placing the index or middle finger over either of the carotid arteries in the lower neck just above the collar bone. Don't apply too much pressure with your fingers, as this will slow the flow of blood to your brain and may induce a sudden drop in heart rate. The radial pulse is found by placing the index and middle fingers on the underside and thumb side of either wrist. Don't take your pulse with your thumb because you have a pulse in your thumb and won't get an accurate count.

After exercising about 10 minutes, take a heart rate test. Take your pulse for 10 seconds, but keep moving quietly but steadily while taking your pulse. Take this number and multiply it by 6 to determine your beats per minute. If this number falls within your training zone, you're aerobic and burning fat. If you're under the lower number, speed up your workout a bit. If you are over the higher number, slow down. Remember that exceeding 85% of your Maximum Heart Rate will not help you to burn fat. Fat burning requires oxygen. If you're over 85% of your MHR, you're out of oxygen and not burning fat.

THE WORKOUTS

1. THE FRENZIED PERSON

Every little bit of exercise counts. It's really true that walking up stairs or walking from the farthest parking spot can help you achieve better cardiovascular fitness. Research has shown that even just a little bit of exercise throughout the day adds toward better fitness.

Here are some simple suggestions to add exercise into your hurried life-style:
- Park your car in the farthest spot from your destination and walk the extra steps.
- Instead of calling a person by phone, walk to their office or home if they're close by.
- Walk to the farthest restroom, coffee pot, breakroom, cafeteria or soda machine.
- Take an energy break and walk for 10 minutes during the day.
- Take a stretch break.
- Eat lunch at your desk and take a walk for the remainder of your lunch break.
- Take advantage of free time on the weekends by adding small blocks of walking—10 to 20 minutes.

These suggestions may seem small, but adding these can add real fitness benefits.

2. THE PERSON WITH MINIMAL TIME

If you can add 20 to 30 minute exercise segments for three nonconsecutive days per week, you can gain a new level of fitness and might achieve some weight loss as well.

Think of this as making an appointment with yourself. People always seem to find time to fit other people and priorities into their schedule, but never include themselves as a priority. MAKE THIS YOUR PRIORITY!

Here are some 30-minute routine examples:

Example Routine 1
- **Aerobic Training**—15 minutes. Gradually warm up, workout for the rest of the 15 minutes within your Target Training Zone. You can spend the entire time on one piece of equipment or use several. Or simply do non-equipment activities such as walking.
- **Strength Training**—10 minutes. Perform a variety of body weight exercises, such as push-ups, dips, etc. and floor exercises, such as leg lifts, crunches, etc.
- **Flexibility Training**—5 minutes. Complete the workout with stretches for all the major muscle groups.

Example Routine 2—at the club, gym or on your own equipment.
- **Warm up**—5 minutes. Perform any cardio activity on any piece of equipment.

• 150 •

- **Flexibility Training**—5 minutes. Briefly stretch all of the major muscle groups.
- **Circuit Training**—15 minutes. Progress from one weight machine to the next, performing 15 to 20 repetitions at each station and quickly moving onto the next station. You can alternate between strength-training and cardiovascular sessions.
- **Cool down**—5 minutes. Gently walk or cycle.

Example Routine 3

- Integrate play or sporting activities into your fitness routine. These may include biking, tennis, racquetball or basketball. Remember to include warm-up and flexibility exercises before and after the activity.

3. THE PERSON WHO CAN MAKE THE TIME

Included here are one-hour example routines for you who have committed to one hour of exercise, 3 to 6 days a week.

Example Routine 1

- **Warm up**—10 minutes. Gently perform an aerobic activity such as walking or cycling.
- **Aerobic Training**—20 to 30 minutes. Focus on one or more cardiovascular activities.
- **Strength Training**—10 to 20 minutes. Perform a variety of body weight and floor exercises, or use strength training equipment.
- **Flexibility Training**—10 minutes. Completely stretch all the major muscle groups.

Example Routine 2
- **Warm up**—10 minutes. Gently perform an aerobic activity such as walking or cycling.
- **Circuit Training**—40 minutes. Progress from one weight machine to the next, performing 15 to 20 repetitions at each station and quickly moving on to the next station. You may alternate between strength-training and cardiovascular stations.
- **Flexibility Training**—10 minutes. Completely stretch all the major muscle groups.

Example Routine 3
- Follow an aerobic training videotape which includes an aerobic activity and strength training. This can be a good motivator and an excellent source for proper training techniques.

Exercise is critical to health and well-being. It doesn't need to be complicated or difficult, either. All it takes is commitment. Most of us have a hard time figuring out how to make time for fitness—whether we're frenzied or even if we've made the time. These few suggestions may help you to integrate an exercise regimen that you can live with.

Remember the Fitness Triangle—cardiovascular training, weight training and flexibility training—is the essence of all fitness programs, no matter how much or little time you have. Try to add these into your lifestyle. And remember, every little bit helps. You will increase your fitness level by doing just a little training.

Chapter Six

Wrap-Up:
This is not the end, but just the beginning...

Awareness is the first step toward change. In this book I've written for you, I hope I've created an awareness that the average real person with a real life like me—overscheduled and overcommitted—can balance cooking healthy, good tasting food with precious time left over to do other things. So you see, if I can do it, *you can, too.*

Let this book be your personal blueprint to create a healthier life-style. Food provides both the energy and the nutrients needed to build and maintain body cells. Nutrients are the nourishing substances found in food. Therefore, it's true—YOU ARE WHAT YOU EAT!

Giving that wonderful body of yours the proper fuel it needs begins with you and the choices you make. You can be the wizard in your own kitchen, stirring up and creating wellness while having the time to enjoy it. Your kitchen is your own territory—you're in control. Your kitchen can be your gateway to wellness.

This book is a reaction to the haunting cries of my clients telling me that they have no time, no energy—and therefore, they're eating garbage and becoming fed up with it! This book helps you change all that.

LET'S KEEP IT SIMPLE

- **The Problem:** You want to eat good healthy food, but you're too tired and don't have enough time to cook.
- **The Solution**: Cook when your energy level is up—probably on the weekend, when you can find an hour or two. Cooking and freezing a moderate quantity of food means having something ready to reheat for almost a month. Or cooking and refrigerating can translate to reheating healthy food for a week and a half.
- **Result:** 20 minutes from freezer or fridge to table.
- **Recap:** Cook when your energy level is up. Freeze and reheat when you're ready to eat.

Once again, here's the *Kitchen Express* formula: One to two hours preparing healthy, fresh food equals almost a month's worth of meals. Once the food has been prepared and stored, you can take advantage of the **20-Minute-Meal Deal**—20 minutes from storage to table. This translates into hours of free time, healthier food alternatives and better self esteem.

LET'S REVIEW WHAT YOU'VE LEARNED IN THIS BOOK.

- Chapter One: How to cook good food fast and the tools you need to do it.
- Chapter Two: Basic, common-sense nutrition, not a lot of jargon. Just the basic facts, giving you knowledge, which gives you power.
- Chapter Three: Smart shopping tips, making the supermarket a more user-friendly place. And Dee's Picks—my favorite products, low fat but tasty.
- Chapter Four: My recipe selections, easy and speedy, low to moderate in fat, and absolutely delicious. Guiltless, healthy eating without sacrificing taste or time.
- Chapter Five: Practical exercise suggestions for even the most harried among us. Exercise is an important key to overall wellness and YOU CAN find time with one of the three plans I present just for you.

Think of this book as your ticket on the *Kitchen Express*. This train ride is the beginning of a journey to greater wellness in your life. You'll not only become great in your own kitchen, you'll also apply a strategy for better living—creating more time for yourself and your loved ones, cooking and eating healthier foods, finding the satisfaction of making something yourself—which leads to an overall feeling of well-being.

Most of all, it's my hope that this book empowers you. You control when you cook, the cleanliness, the ingredients and the cost of food. You are the wizard that makes your kitchen a safe haven from fatty, chemical-laden processed and fast foods.

• 156 •

I hope you've enjoyed your journey on the *KITCHEN EXPRESS*. But this trip doesn't ever have to end—the *Kitchen Express* will always keep you on the right tract to healthy eating, more free time, and a happier, healthier life-style. Empower yourself—take a lifetime ticket—get a permanent seat on your very own **Kitchen Express**.

Happy, healthy cooking and more free time! All the Best!

Recipe Index

Appetizers
- Gamekeeper's Cold Shrimp with Fruit 58
- Garlic-Y White Bean Spread 56
- Horsy Shrimp Dip 54

Apple Squares 132

Applesauce Parfait, Yogurt 130

Chicken "Sloppy Dee's" 110

Cranberry Relish, Garnet 60

Dee's Magic Mix 62

Dee's No-Fried Breaded Chicken Breasts 100

Dee's Ratatouille 80

Desserts
- Apple Squares 132
- "Pudding on the Ritz" Lemon Mousse 134
- Yogurt Applesauce Parfait 130

Effortless Roasted Herbed Chicken 106

Eggplant Tapinade, 20-Minute Vegetarian 82

Fat Free Garlic Mashed Potatoes 88

Gamekeeper's Cold Shrimp Appetizer 58

Garlic-Y White Bean Spread 56

Garnet Cranberry Relish 60

Grilled Chicken Breasts 102

Grilled Turkey 114

Hearty -Hearty Vegetable Beef Soup 72

Herbed Baked Sweet Potatoes 92

Horsy Shrimp Dip 54

Lamb, Roasted Leg of 118

Lasagna, Vegetable 76

Lean Marinated Roast Pork Loin 122

Lean Rump Roast 124

Lemon Chicken 104

Lemon Mousse, "Pudding on the Ritz" 134

Low Fat Pasta Sensation 94

Marsha's Chicken Chili 70

Meat Loaf, Sunday Turkey 116

Milli-G's Vegetable Cakes 84

Molonari's Chicken with Portobello Mushrooms 108

No-Fat Whipped Spinach Potatoes 90

Pasta
- Sauce (meatless), Versatile Basil 78
- Sensation, Low Fat 94
- Sensation Zucchini Variation 96

Pork Loin, Lean Marinated Roast 122

Potatoes
- and Vegetables, Skillet 86
- Fat Free Garlic Mashed 88
- Herbed Baked Sweet 92
- No-Fat Whipped Spinach 90

Poultry
- Chicken "Sloppy Dee's" 110
- Dee's No-Fried Breaded Chicken Breasts 100
- Effortless Roasted Herbed Chicken 105
- Grilled Chicken Breasts 102
- Grilled Turkey 114
- Lemon Chicken 104
- Low Fat Pasta Sensation 94
- Marsha's Chicken Chili 70

Molonari's Chicken with Portobello Mushrooms 108
Quick Open Face Main Meal Sandwich 120
Roasted Turkey Breast 112
Sunday Turkey Meat Loaf 116
Quick Open Face Main Meal Sandwich 120
Roast, Lean Rump 124
Roasted Leg of Lamb 118
Roasted Turkey Breast 112
Sauce, Versatile Basil Pasta (meatless) 78
Seafood
    Gamekeeper's Cold Shrimp Appetizer 58
    Horsy Shrimp Dip 54
    Shrimp Creole 74

Seasoning
    Dee's Magic Mix 62
Shrimp Appetizer, Gamekeeper's Cold 58
Shrimp Creole 74
Skillet Potatoes and Vegetables 86
Soups
    Hearty-Hearty Vegetable Beef 72
    Shrimp Creole 74
Sunday Turkey Meat Loaf 116
Sweet Potatoes, Herbed Baked 92
Tuna Cakes 126
Turkey
    Breast, Roasted 112

    Grilled 114
    Meat Loaf, Sunday 116
    Quick Open Face Main Meal Sandwich 120
Twenty-Minute Vegetarian Eggplant Tapinade 82
Vegetables
    20-Minute Vegetarian Eggplant Tapinade 82
    Cakes, Milli-G's 84
    Dee's Ratatouille 80
    Lasagna 76
    Skillet Potatoes and 86
Versatile Basil Pasta Sauce (meatless) 78
Yogurt Applesauce Parfait 130
Zucchini Variation, Pasta Sensation 96

Order Additional Copies—Only $12.95 Each

Kitchen Express makes an excellent gift for today's schedule-driven individual who wants to provide good nutrition for the family, but has little time to prepare it. Sound familiar? Buy several copies to keep on hand when you want to give a useful gift that will be appreciated for simplifying day-to-day living.

Send a check or money order for $12.95 each plus $2.50 postage for any amount of books ordered to:

Quail Ridge Press
P. O. Box 123
Brandon, MS 39043

Call toll-free to order by credit card or to request a free catalog of all Quail Ridge Press titles. Wholesalers call for quantity discount terms.

1-800-343-1583

More Health-Conscious Titles from Quail Ridge Press

Eat Your Way Thin • 104 pages • ringbound • $9.95
Lite Up Your Life • 304 pages • ringbound • $14.95
Reset Your Appestat • 200 pages • hardcover • $12.95
AgeLess: Living Younger Longer • 208 pages • hardcover • $14.95

More Cookbooks from Quail Ridge Press

The Complete Venison Cookbook • 432 pages • paperbound • $19.95
Best of Bayou Cuisine • 288 pages • ringbound • $14.95
The Little Gumbo Book • 64 pages • hardcover • $8.95
Hors D'Oeuvres Everybody Loves • 80 pages • ringbound • $5.95